NEATNESS COUNTS

NEATNESS COUNTS
Essays on the Writer's Desk

Kevin Kopelson

University of Minnesota Press – Minneapolis – London

The publication of this book was assisted by a bequest from Josiah H. Chase to honor his parents, Ellen Rankin Chase and Josiah Hook Chase, Minnesota territorial pioneers.

Published by the University of Minnesota Press
111 Third Avenue South, Suite 290
Minneapolis, MN 55401-2520
http://www.upress.umn.edu

Library of Congress Cataloging-in-Publication Data

Kopelson, Kevin, 1960–
    Neatness counts : essays on the writer's desk / Kevin Kopelson.
       p.   cm.
    Includes bibliographical references and index.
    ISBN 0-8166-4401-2 (hc/j : alk. paper)
    1. Literature, Modern—20th century—History and criticism.
  2. Orderliness. 3. Authorship—Psychological aspects.   I. Title.
    PN770.5.K67 2004
    809'.03—dc22

                             2004010415

Printed in the United States of America on acid-free paper

The University of Minnesota is an equal-opportunity educator and employer.

12 11 10 09 08 07 06 05 04   10 9 8 7 6 5 4 3 2 1

For David Coster

JEAN-LOUIS DE RAMBURES: Do you have a method of working?

ROLAND BARTHES: It all depends on what you mean by method. As far as methodology is concerned, I have no opinion. But if you're talking about work habits, obviously I have a method of working. And on that basis your question interests me, because there is a kind of censorship that considers this topic taboo, under the pretext that it would be futile for a writer or an intellectual to talk about his writing, his daily schedule, or his desk.

—*Roland Barthes, "An Almost Obsessive Relation to Writing Instruments"*

CONTENTS

ACKNOWLEDGMENTS

THIS WORK, prompted by Dee Morris and Bob Scholes, has been supported by the University of Iowa, the Radcliffe Institute for Advanced Study at Harvard University, the Camargo Foundation, various girlfriends (Meredith Alexander, Paola Bacchetta, Tina Bourjaily, Michèle Côme, Jennifer Doyle, Carolyn Fay, Kim Marra, Diane Middlebrook, Geeta Patel, Lorry Perry, and Angela Voos), and imaginary boyfriends (Joe Boone, Pierre-Paul Casabianca, Bill Cohen, Chris Gaggero, Charles Hawley, Wayne Koestenbaum, Tom Lutz, Jesse Matz, Eve Kosofsky Sedgwick, Maxim Shrayer, Downing Thomas, and Doug Trevor).

INTRODUCTION

I SHARED MY FIRST DESK WITH MY BROTHER STEVE, a rickety affair our father made out of an old headboard. We did grade school homework there—nothing memorable. I did housework, too, because the finches I kept nearby left it messy.

Steve got our brother Eric's desk when Eric wandered off to California. I got brother Bob's. But the drawers still contained their stuff, including index cards covered with quotations from writers like Dostoyevsky, Rilke, and Proust. (Imagine Zooey Glass perusing the bedroom walls his oldest brothers, Seymour and Buddy, had covered with Kafka.) In addition to junior high and high school homework, I myself wrote fiction there—all of it terrible, of course, and only one story I can recall with any specificity: something about brothers who build a house of cards that represents something or other. All I can recall of the desktop is the gunmetal blue desk set and a manual typewriter that never worked very well.

I didn't write fiction in college, where my school supplied the furniture. I wrote term papers and poetry—terrible, formless love poetry. Plus a pretty good sestina, after Elizabeth Bishop, about playing the piano.[1] All I can recall of those desktops is an electric typewriter that, in addition to not working very well, weighed a ton.

I didn't need a desk in law school (where I lived off campus) because I didn't have to write much. I did have a kitchen table, which is where I must have written those course outlines. (Neatness counts.) I'm less sure about letters, which I may have done in bed.

I did need a desk as a lawyer, of course. I even needed one at home, where I preferred to work as much as possible. I bought an ugly modern one with a secret compartment, not knowing, ironically enough, that I did have something to hide. The law firm fired me for being gay, which was legal at the time. I also began a novel there, a confessional narrative I discarded a long time ago and only one line of which, about a sexual encounter, comes to mind: "My body embarrassed me." Having discarded the electric typewriter even longer ago, I wrote the thing by hand. The only item on the desktop: an incandescent lamp Dad gave me.

I wrote my first book, a Barthesian dissertation on "modern homoerotics," at the same desk but in another home and on my first computer. (I'd left law for literary criticism.) The only other item on the desktop: a halogen lamp I took from the firm. I wrote my second book, Barthesian essays on "pianism," at the same desk and on the same computer but in yet another home. (I'd been hired by a university to teach "queer theory.") The only other item on the desktop: another incandescent lamp I bought when I got the job. I wrote my third, Barthesian essays on Nijinsky, in a

---

1. Asked whether college students do traditional forms well, Bishop replied, "I don't know. We did a sestina—we started one in class by drawing words out of a hat—and I wish I'd never suggested it because it seemed to have *swept* Harvard. Later in the applications for my class, I'd get dozens of sestinas. The students seemed to think it was my favorite form—which it isn't" (quoted in Spires, 70, emphasis original).

messy friend's home, at a folding card table cleared of his debris, once again, the computer having died, by hand. (I'd been given a residential fellowship where Marc lived.) I'm writing this book on a new, portable computer at two different but equally uncluttered desks. One is the beautiful *bureau-plat* I bought when I got tenure. (No more secret compartments.) The other, a rolltop, is my beautiful partner's. David and I share separate homes.

This book is about the poetics of the desk, a subject Bachelard— notwithstanding his interest in related areas such as drawers and "nests"—fails to address in *The Poetics of Space*.[2] Nor, to my knowledge, do any Anglo-American critics speak to it.[3] What do desks represent for writers? How do writers represent desks? For whom does the topography of the desk correspond to the topography of literary creation? For whom does it not correspond? I hope my brief autobibliography has suggested some of the reasons—or at least the main reason—I'm drawn to these and related questions: I find it hard to understand how some people find disorder productive. I also hope it indicates my idiosyncratic, impressionistic approach. (Instead of attempting a comprehensive, conventionally rigorous analysis, I'll simply discuss several twentieth-century authors I like a lot: a poet, a novelist, a critic, a playwright, and a travel writer. With Bishop, the poet, I address the cluttered desk; with Proust, the novelist, the nestlike desk, or writing in bed; with Roland Barthes, the schematic desk, or structural idiosyncrasy; with Tom Stoppard, the dramatic desk, or structural irony; with Bruce Chatwin—let's just say I used *"bureau-plat"* for a reason.) It's the kind of writing I find most pleasurable, the kind of formal

---

2. See Barthes, *Pleasure of the Text,* 37: "For Bachelard, it seems that writers have never written: by a strange lacuna, they are only read. Thus he has been able to establish a pure critique of reading, and he has grounded it in pleasure. . . . But once the work is perceived in terms of a *writing,* pleasure balks, bliss appears, and Bachelard withdraws" (emphasis original).

3. See Schehr, however, for a superb discussion of Flaubert. See also Fuss. For historical looks at the male writer's study, see Chartier, Nancy (on Descartes), Ophir (on Montaigne), and Thornton. For one such look at the female writer's desk, see Pelz. For a coffee-table book on various writers' work space, see Drucker and Lerner. For various writers' remarks on their own work habits, see Krementz. For writers' remarks on rooms of their own other than the study, see Fiffer and Fiffer. For remarks on their sense of home, see Doty.

challenge I find most compelling, and the kind of intellectual exhibition I find least, well, embarrassing. Why this should be so is, I confess, a bit of a mystery. All I know is that I learned the approach from Barthes, a mentor who happens—or pretends—not to believe in "authors" or to consider himself intellectual and who, like me, is decidedly *un*decided about psychoanalysis. (I've learned quotation technique from both J. D. Salinger and Walter Benjamin.) So, in a way, *Neatness Counts* is also all about him. And in a different way, about my brother Steve—something else I've tried to indicate. But it's *for* David, who among other attributes, like making space and keeping birds of his own, happens to believe in me.

DESK WORK

Not "to know" but to schematize—to impose upon chaos as
much regularity and form as our practical needs require.
—*Nietzsche*, The Will to Power

MARY MCCARTHY says she wouldn't call her friend Elizabeth
Bishop a great writer; she'd call her "neat." Willard Spiegelman
agrees, calling Bishop "fastidious" (203). They must mean her
poems, because the woman who wrote them wasn't neat at all.
Bishop had a messy study and even messier desk, which she says
bothered her.[1]

(Of course, some find neatness masculine—not to mention
anal. Female writing, they say, is slovenly. So are female anatomy
and psychology. Degas's women, for example, signify both sexual
and emotional mess. Male writing, however—well, ponder what
Mary Orr says about Flaubert, whose prose she calls masculine

---

1. See Spires, 58. See also Mead, 48: Auden hated living in disorder as well but told
Edmund Wilson (McCarthy's husband) that it was the only way he could work.

1

not because of its "muscular style" but because of its "phobic response to disorder" [206]. Of course, even superficially chaotic, associative work can be profoundly organized, just as anatomical distortions in Ingres make sense on a linear level and individual anomalies contribute to the formal resolution of the whole.)[2]

So why didn't Bishop clean up her desk? Shouldn't the creation of orderly verse require domestic order? And if that creation required disorder, why be bothered by it? The poems themselves provide the answer. So does "12 O'Clock News," a prose poem originally called "News Report [From the Desk]." (By "originally," I mean forty years prior to completion. No other poet took so long to finalize work.)[3] In it, Bishop describes the writer's desk as would a war correspondent describing some foreign battleground: A gooseneck lamp is a moon that "seems to hang motionless in the sky"; some envelopes, signboards "on a truly gigantic scale"; an ink bottle, an altar "to which, in their present historical state of superstition and helplessness, [the people] attribute magical powers"; an ashtray, a "nest" of soldiers clearly seen from a "superior vantage point" (*Complete Poems,* 174–75).[4] (No desk of hers, whether real or imaginary, seems to have had drawers.) To cite consecutive sections:

typewriter
The escarpment that rises abruptly from the central plain is in heavy shadow, but the elaborate terracing of its southern glacis gleams faintly in the dim light, like fish scales. What endless labor those small, peculiarly shaped terraces represent! And yet, on them the welfare of this tiny principality depends.

pile of mss.
A slight landslide occurred in the northwest about an hour ago. The exposed soil appears to be of poor quality: almost white, calcareous, and shaly. There are believed to have been no casualties.

---

2. See Freud, "Character and Anal Eroticism," 27, 28. See also Callen, 98; Ockman, 87; and Vigne, 76.
3. Both "News Report [From the Desk]" and "12 O'Clock News" literalize the metonymy "news desk." "News Report," however, is in rhymed verse. See Monteiro, 89.
4. All further citations of Bishop's poetry in this chapter are from *Complete Poems.*

typed sheet

Almost due north, our aerial reconnaissance reports the discovery of a large rectangular "field," hitherto unknown to us, obviously man-made. It is dark-speckled. An airstrip? A cemetery? (174)

Needless to say, this is ludicrous. "12 O'Clock News" is satirizing a kind of journalism we don't see anymore: woefully misinformed but wonderfully articulate. Yet an even messier poet, James Merrill, found it Bishop's saddest poem, probably because—despite Bishop's efforts to distance the "news" desk from her own, at which poems were done by hand (typewriters are for letter writing) and on which alcoholic beverages were part of the scenery as well—it also represents the lonely agony of literary creation: the desktop a battleground in which rejected drafts and cigarettes aren't the only casualties.[5] Sadder—presumably due to self-directed irony—than "The Man-Moth," her other nocturne on the alienated artist ("He thinks the moon is a small hole at the top of the sky" [14]). Sadder, even, than her poems on premature loss: "Crusoe in England" ("Pretty to watch; he had a pretty body" [166]), "One Art" ("I lost two cities, lovely ones" [178]), and "Sestina" (*Time to plant tears, says the almanac* [124, emphasis original]).[6]

I find Bishop's "superior vantage point" significant. She frequently imagines landscapes, usually seashores, from high above. (She also imagines inverted overviews: "It is so peaceful on the ceiling! / It is the Place de la Concorde. / The little crystal chandelier / is off, the fountain is in the dark. / Not a soul is in the park" ["Sleeping on the Ceiling," 29].) This occurs in "In the Village," a prose poem about losing her demented mother.[7] (No one hears the

---

5. See Millier, 474.

6. Bishop—an only child—lost both parents at a young age and was raised by relatives, both rich and poor. In "The Country Mouse," she recalls her paternal grandfather's opulent study: "In the library there were some bookcases filled with dark leather-bound books, but I was the only one who ever used it. After two months or so of my sojourn, I got up my courage and slid open the glass doors. The carpet was a deep rich blue. There was a mahogany desk in the middle of the room, with a brass desk set and a paperweight in the form of three lifelike bronze cigars. It was heavy, but I picked it up many times and found it smelled of metal, not cigars" (Bishop, *Collected Prose*, 26).

7. For the child of such a mother, notes Marilyn Lombardi, "sanity was linked with the surface securities of an undisturbed domestic life—'peaceful ceilings,' wall-papered walls, unmarked writing paper, and a tidy desk" (186).

echo of a scream hanging over that Nova Scotian village, but you can hear it by flicking a lightning rod on top of the church "with your fingernail" [*Collected Prose,* 251].) It occurs in "Roosters," a war poem:

> A rooster gloats
>
> over our beds
> from rusty iron sheds
> and fences made from old bedsteads,
>
> over our churches
> where the tin rooster perches,
> over our little wooden northern houses,
>
> making sallies
> from all the muddy alleys,
> marking out maps like Rand McNally's. (36)

It also occurs in "The Map," "The Unbeliever," "Argument," "The Burglar of Babylon," "Going to the Bakery," "Night City [From the Plane]," and "Pleasure Seas." (These do feature seashores: "Land lies in water; it is shadowed green" ["The Map," 3]; "He sleeps on the top of a mast / with his eyes fast closed" ["The Unbeliever," 22]; "Remember all that land / beneath the plane; / that coastline / of dim beaches deep in sand" ["Argument," 81]; "Far, far below, the people / were little colored spots, / And the heads of those in swimming / were floating coconuts" ["The Burglar of Babylon," 116]; "Instead of gazing at the sea / the way she does on other nights, the moon looks down the Avenida / Copacabana at the sights, // new to her but ordinary" ["Going to the Bakery," 151]; "The city burns tears. / A gathered lake / of aquamarine / begins to smoke" ["Night City {From the Plane}," 167]; "Happy the people in the swimming-pool and on the yacht, / Happy the man in that airplane, likely as not" ["Pleasure Seas," 196].)

Bishop did live in high places with spectacular views: on mountains with waterfalls, in waterfront apartments. Her mountain home—shared with Lota de Macedo Soares—was in Petrópolis, Brazil. Her apartments were in both Rio de Janeiro and—after

Lota's suicide—Boston, Massachussetts.[8] As an asthma sufferer, moreover, she did spend a lot of time in bed—presumably looking out of windows, or up at ceilings, and reading. (Proust had asthma too, but spent his bed time otherwise.) Yet the frequency with which Bishop imagines littoral views from above should also be attributed to a predilection for the cartographer's global perspective: for seeing the big picture, or for representing large things on a small scale. (Bishop told Marianne Moore that the roosters—in "Roosters"—are placed here and there by their various crowings "like the pins that point out war projects on a map" [*One Art*, 96].)[9] This predilection, however, exists in tension with one for the painter's, if not the neatnik's, eye for detail.[10] Or even for another bird's eye: Bishop's "Sandpiper," who, instead of conducting aerial reconnaissance, runs along the shoreline "watching his toes":

> —Watching, rather, the spaces of sand between them,
> where (no detail too small) the Atlantic drains
> rapidly backwards and downwards. As he runs,
> he stares at the dragging grains. (131)

"12 O'Clock News" is one of only three works in which Bishop presents both predilections at once: seeing small things—a lamp, a typewriter—up close and in detail yet as if from afar. ("The elaborate terracing of its southern glacis gleams faintly in the dim light, like fish scales.") The others are "Sleeping on the Ceiling" and "A Miracle for Breakfast." These clearly demonstrate that this tension involves both metaphor and misrecognition—or construing such things as large: the lamp, the moon; the typewriter, an escarpment. (In "Sleeping on the Ceiling," Bishop sees her chandelier as

---

8. Bishop ends "One Art" with the suicide: "—Even losing you (the joking voice, a gesture / I love) I shan't have lied. It's evident / the art of losing's not too hard to master / though it may look like (*Write* it!) like disaster" (179).
9. The explanation is both defensive and aggressive. Moore would have revised and retitled "Roosters," calling it "The Cock." In rejecting this advice, Bishop signaled the end of an apprenticeship. See Kalstone, 79–85, 265–69.
10. See Bishop, "The U.S.A. School of Writing," in *Collected Prose*, 46: The primitive painter "lingers" over detail, emphasizing it at the expense of the picture as a whole.

a fountain. In "A Miracle for Breakfast," she sees a breadcrumb as a mansion.) The poet knows—wants us to know, or to know she knows—that cartographers miss the details, and painters the big picture; or that you can't see very well if you're both farsighted and nearsighted, right-brained and left-brained, global and local.[11] Unless, of course, you're Leonardo da Vinci. Or Proust, perhaps. Or maybe Bishop herself on a good day, to credit "12 O'Clock News" despite its delusional and even self-promotional aspects. Great writing does resolve the tension.

Why then is there no water here? Bishop's "tiny principality" seems landlocked because her desktop also represents unfamiliar territory. For the poet, who, having spent her childhood near the Atlantic, felt grounded by the sea, the field of inquiry—whether war zone or exotic landscape—is one in which she is not at home.[12] Like many writers, she finds the field uncanny (*unheimlich,* "unhomely"). This is to say, however, that she finds it eerily familiar as well. Unrecognizable (or misrecognizable) yet secretly recognizable (or so she hopes), disorganized yet secretly organized (perhaps), it is a space in which conceptual tidiness may lurk somewhere out of sight, out of mind—possibly unconscious.[13] (Freud associates *Heimlichkeit* with the "careful housewife" who conceals things ["The Uncanny," 155].) If she's lucky, it's a place where the comforting shoreline of familiarity is just beyond the horizon or over the edge.

Why then, despite the messiness of Bishop's desk, does the unfamiliar "news" desk seem remarkably neat? Why, when hers had books, papers, and magazines piled everywhere, is the only sign of disorder that somewhat disheveled pile of manuscripts? ("A *slight* landslide occurred in the northwest about an hour ago" [emphasis

---

11. To schematize our in fact rather chaotic neural organization: The right hemisphere is associated with disorder, spontaneity, the big picture, and the unconscious; the left hemisphere with order, discipline, detail, consciousness, and language. Somewhat counterintuitively, the right hemisphere is also associated with poetry, the left with prose. Then again, the right hemisphere is the one that tracks sound.

12. See Stevenson, *Five Looks at Elizabeth Bishop,* 125: Speaking as a journalist in "a strange, embattled country," Bishop describes "a secret landscape not unlike the exile's island colonized by Crusoe." My point, however, is that the country doesn't seem like an island.

13. See Vendler on Bishop and the uncanny. See also McCabe, 210; and Lombardi, 177–78, 180, 194–95.

added].) Because unlike the ink bottle or the ashtray, the manuscripts are, in fact, Bishop's attempts to make sense of senselessness. The manuscripts are poems, presumably, but possibly letters
as well. The unproductive poet was a voluminous letter writer,
largely a function of geographic isolation: years lived in Florida,
years and years in Brazil. Insofar as they're poems, I'm thinking
of how each one looks or sounds as well as what it says: senselessness as a mess of signifiers as well as signifieds. And so the sign is
no anomaly. To the extent it's a mess, the manuscript pile is both
metonymy for Bishop's desk, on which it happens to rest, and
metaphor for the senselessness against which she struggled. To the
extent it's a *tidy* mess (like the "news" desk on which it also rests),
the pile is both metaphor and metonymy for each manuscript
therein, both metaphor and metonymy for the struggle itself.

I should say more about signifieds. For Bishop, writing and
thinking are the same process, which is why she didn't write poetry
at the keyboard. ("This machine types faster than I can think,"
she told one correspondent, "and I'm afraid this [letter] shows
it" [*One Art,* 553].) Nor should her poetry pretend to be anything
else, as we know from the many hesitations, self-corrections, self-
interrogations, and suspensions that characterize even final drafts:
successive attempts to neaten up an idea concluded by resolutions
to leave the mess somewhat unresolved. ("Watching his toes. /
—Watching, rather, the spaces of sand between them.") Some
describe this style as the mind "in action" as opposed to repose.
Even Bishop might; she did describe Browning and Hopkins that
way. But given the extensive labor involved in both producing
and polishing these drafts (working with language, form, and
information as well as with the unconscious), the style could be
called letter-like. (There's play involved too, of course, and repose.
"A group of words, a phrase, may find its way into my head like
something floating in the sea, and presently it attracts other things
to it," Bishop admits [quoted in Monteiro, 25].) The "imaginative
ideal" she sought to realize in verse was, in fact, the "studied spontaneity and 'mediated immediacy'" of correspondence (Hammer,
164, 178). That ideal, moreover, indicates the labor involved far
more than the play. Bishop's rigor: the tidy mess of studied spontaneity (as well as controlled disorder) found in the work itself and

in the thoroughly disordered work space neatened up a bit, if only in fantasy, by "12 O'Clock News."

The neatening up was, in fact, a fantasy. As Bishop wrote to Robert Lowell from Florida:

> The harbor [Garrison Bight in Key West] is always a mess, here, junky little boats all piled up, some hung with sponges and always a few half sunk or splintered up from the most recent hurricane. It reminds me a little of my desk. (*One Art,* 154)

I read that final line as a complaint, one basis of my initial assertion that domestic disorder bothered Bishop. The reading itself is supported by other correspondence in which Bishop describes such disorder, or "chaos," as "appalling."[14] It's also supported by a letter to Merrill in which, with ironic reference to Octavio Paz, Bishop writes, "I must say my glimpse of *his* desk & study—after he had lived in their new apartment for 2 weeks—helped me a lot. It looks even worse than mine does after 2 years here—but then, he's a *very* important gentleman" (*One Art,* 582, emphasis original).

Bishop versifies that harbor in "The Bight," a letter-like work in which her book, paper, magazine, and letter–littered desk appears via a metaphorical "correspondence" to correspondence—pun intended, as is the Baudelaire reference:[15]

> Some of the little white boats are still piled up
> against each other, or lie on their sides, stove in,
> and not yet salvaged, if they ever will be, from the last bad storm,

---

14. See, e.g., Bishop, *One Art,* 523, 529.
15. See Levinson, 209–10: "In 'The Bight,' another defining poem for Bishop, Baudelaire's poetics of 'correspondence' is invoked as a model for Bishop's own aesthetic. The allusion is as useful for the differences it brings out as it is for the identities. In Baudelaire, a controlling consciousness lodges in the very idiom of the writing: a highly inflected, socially placeable lexicon, tonality, and drift of desire. By contrast, Bishop's correspondences are left to speak for themselves; they are not subjected to a grammar of motive, an atmospheric intelligence, or anything else that might mobilize them in the direction of statement or character. Bishop's free-floating analogies, echoes, and couplings are offered neither as objectively grounded relations, 'released' by the mechanisms of the poem or derived from some metaphysical source; nor are they presented as artifacts contrived by an agency that is textualized in the poem. As a rule, resemblance in Bishop acts as an inscrutably first and formal cause, responsible for the narrative movement and conceptual designs that emerge from the poem."

like torn-open, unanswered letters.
The bight is littered with old correspondences.
Click. Click. Goes the dredge,
and brings up a dripping jawful of marl.
All the untidy activity continues,
awful but cheerful. (60–61)

For Spiegelman, this conclusion concerning the idea of disorder at Key West is meant as self-critique: Bishop "is looking at herself through the veil of the scene before her" (209). In her understated way, he explains, "she has dramatized as if unconsciously the 'untidy activity' not merely of a dredge or a single natural scene but of a whole world which includes the speaker and her attempt to perceive or impose beauty around her" (211). True enough. But given the ways Bishop was haunted by it—and even wished that we be—I prefer to see the conclusion as a critical, possibly inspirational motto. (We all have them. Mine is "True enough.") Shortly after "The Bight" appeared in the *New Yorker,* Bishop told a doctor who treated both her asthma and her alcoholism, "I wrote it last year but I still think if I can just keep the last line in mind ["awful but cheerful"], everything may still turn out all right" (*One Art,* 184). Twenty years later, in San Francisco, she taught a mynah bird to say "awful but cheerful." She also taught it "I, too, dislike it," a line of Moore's on poetry, and "Nobody knows," a line of her maternal grandmother's. (The mysterious remark "was a sort of chorus in our lives," notes Bishop. "'Nobody knows . . . *nobody knows . . .*' I often wondered what my grandmother knew and if she alone knew it, or if it was a total mystery that really nobody knew except perhaps God. I even asked her, '*What* do you know, Gammie, that we don't know? Why don't you tell us? Tell me!'" ["Memories of Uncle Neddy," in *Collected Prose,* 241–42, emphasis and ellipses original].) Ten years after that, she arranged to have "awful but cheerful" inscribed on her tombstone. But it wasn't.[16]

That the "awful," messy activity is "cheerful" as well and not, say, "fruitful" or (less poetic) "productive" indicates that it helped Bishop combat depression—depression associated with alcoholism,

16. See Millier, 406, 550.

isolation, the isolation of the activity itself (writing), idleness (not writing), and loss. Or that she hoped it helped. Writing, after all, can be pleasurable. Blissful even, to cite Barthes. So can making sense—finding or creating order, perceiving or imposing beauty—whether in writing, thinking, or otherwise. Blocked? Clean up your room.[17] Bishop, aptly enough, first versified cleaning her shoes. "Her own beginnings as a poet go back to the age of eight," writes George Monteiro.

> Miss Bishop remembers a morning when her grandmother, preparing her for Sunday school, was sprucing up her shoes. The shoes were patent leather with white tops. To clean the tops, the grandmother used gasoline, and Vaseline for the patent leather. The little girl was intoxicated by the rhyme. "I went around all day chanting 'gasoline / Vaseline,'" the older Bishop said. "It may not have been a poem, but it was my first rhyme." (71)

Many writers, including Bishop, think (and write) like chaos theorists. (Such theorists aren't really interested in chaos. Unlike Nietzsche, they're interested in order arising from truly chaotic systems as well as order concealed by seemingly chaotic ones. They're interested, moreover, in the fact that there is no order without chaos. For Nietzsche, of course, there are no "facts"—only interpretations.)[18] Relatively few, however, really work that way. Few, that is, put chaos theory into practice, or materialize it, by keeping a messy work space—unlike more than a few visual artists. Take Degas, for example. "[There's] a connection between the pell-mell state of Degas's studio and the distinctive empiricism of his methods," writes David Trotter: "To live *in* mess is to live *with* mess, and thus to understand that an image occupies the world it would

---

17. See Collins, "Advice to Writers," in *The Apple That Astonished Paris,* 57: "Even if it keeps you up all night, / wash down the walls and scrub the floor / of your study before composing a syllable. // Clean the place as if the Pope were on his way. / Spotlessness is the niece of inspiration. // The more you clean, the more brilliant / your writing will be, so do not hesitate to take / to the open fields to scour the undersides / of rocks or swab in the dark forest / upper branches, nests full of eggs. // When you find your way back home / and stow the sponges and brushes under the sink, / you will behold in the light of dawn / the immaculate altar of your desk, / a clean surface in the middle of a clean world."
18. See Hayles: For chaos theorists, "chaos" simply means complexity; disorder is simply order we don't yet recognize.

bring into representation rather as a person occupies the world he or she would bring into use" (314, emphasis original). As for Ingres, we know both that he craved domestic order and that he couldn't create it himself. In 1807, he complained of having been unable to organize his life when "delivered to my own devices, whether by my own fault or involuntarily," adding that "you see the results in the disorder of my affairs" (quoted in Vigne, 61). Happily, he married a woman who was a wonderful housekeeper. Consider Jean Alaux's *Ingres Studio in Rome* (1818), a painting in which Madeleine Chapelle stands in the foreground, survey-ing the scene of domestic order for which she seems responsible, while Ingres sits in the middle ground, gazing at her apprecia-tively and holding his violin (instead of a brush). Bishop may have materialized chaos theory because she was a painter as well, but also because chaotic desks provide a false sense of productivity.[19] They both indicate and alleviate the anxiety of idleness: I must be busy—just look at this mess![20]

Like Degas, Bishop seems to have been more interested in order arising from chaos than in order concealed by it. Unlike him, how-ever, she also seems to have been interested in order managing— or failing—to contain disorder. Or so I infer both from her equivo-cal attitude toward poetic form and from a formalist reading

---

19. See Goldensohn, 118: "Quite apart from any role that any single painter can be said to have played in [Bishop's] poetry, her connection to picture-making was direct, intense, and prolonged; she was both a maker and a collector of pictures and objects throughout her life."

20. Cf. Gladwell, 93, on this kind of behavior: "The messy desk is not necessarily a sign of disorganization. It may be a sign of complexity: those who deal with many unresolved ideas simultaneously cannot sort and file the papers on their desks, because they haven't yet sorted and filed the ideas in their head." Writers who "live with mess" include Allan Gurganus and Studs Terkel. Gurganus writes, "Where I live becomes partly office supply store, partly a tragicomic thrift shop attempt at creating a little bourgeois comfort, partly alchemist's medicine chest, partly the toy-strewn nursery of a well-equipped if not spoiled child. The place also serves as a Southerner's ancestor-worship altar, a hermit's cave, a telephone clearinghouse, and, whenever possible, a seducer's den. Mostly it's a beloved yeasty petri dish for ideas, friendships, hopes. It is Yeats's 'rag and bone shop of the heart'" (quoted in Fiffer and Fiffer, 222–23). Terkel writes, "Now my desk is a higgledy-piggledy desk. It's disheveled, disheveled as I am in my clothing. I am consistent in what I suppose you would call 'dishevelry.' It's not something deliberate. I'm just organically so. . . . Organic dishevelry: that's how I work, and that's what I am" (quoted in Drucker and Lerner, ix).

of "The Map."[21] In it, the disorderly second stanza concerning
land (unrhymed, with irregular lines) is sandwiched between—or
completely ruptures—the orderly first and third concerning water.
Which interpretation Bishop herself preferred must have depended
on how things seemed to her at the time. If they seemed too orderly,
disorder beckoned; if too disorderly, order did.[22] In the ironic "In
Prison," for example, she imagines comporting herself either neatly
or messily so as to distinguish herself from other inmates. (Prison,
in Bishop's fantasy if not Bourdieu's, isn't *habitus* forming.)

> I shall manage to look just a little different in my uniform
> from the rest of the prisoners. I shall leave the top button of the
> shirt undone, or roll the long sleeves halfway between wrist and
> elbow—something just a little casual, a little Byronic. On the
> other hand, if that is already the general tone in the prison, I
> shall affect a severe, mechanical neatness. My carriage and facial
> expression will be influenced by the same motive. There is, how-
> ever, no insincerity in any of this; it is my conception of my role
> in prison life. It is entirely a different thing from being a "rebel"
> outside the prison; it is to be unconventional, rebellious perhaps,
> but in shades and shadows. (*Collected Prose*, 189)

She imagines writing on the wall this way too:

> Perhaps I shall arrange my "works" in a series of neat inscrip-
> tions in a clear, Roman print; perhaps I shall write them diago-

---

21. Bishop revealed that equivocal attitude to an unidentified correspondent:
"I don't know what 'poetic tools & structures' are, unless you mean traditional
forms. Which one can use or not, as one sees fit. If you feel you are 'moralizing' too
much—just cut the morals off—or out. (Quite often young poets tend to try to tie
everything up neatly in 2 or 3 beautiful last lines, and it is quite surprising how the
poems are improved if the poet can bear to sacrifice those last, pat, beautiful lines.)"
The last line of the letter, a handwritten postscript, reads: "This is a borrowed
machine; please forgive the untidiness" (*One Art*, 596).
22. When Harvard students turned in verse a bit too free on the first day of class,
verse she considered both "awful" and "appalling," Bishop told them, "I'm going
to have to be very strict with you, I see. Let's do something like Housman for the
first assignment. I just want something *neat*—like a hymn" (quoted in Monteiro,
40, emphasis original). When Lowell saw the film *Black Orpheus*, Bishop told him,
"Carnival isn't like that—it's much, much better. For one thing the samba schools
[would] never mix with the crowd. . . . Carnival's one big glorious mess, but a more
orderly and artistic mess, really" (*One Art*, 381).

nally, across a corner, or at the base of a wall and half on the floor, in an almost illegible scrawl. They will be brief, suggestive, anguished, but full of the lights of revelation. And no small part of the joy these writings will give me will be to think of the person coming after me—the legacy of thoughts I shall leave him, like an old bundle tossed carelessly into a corner! (189)

Messy or not, there's no desk in that fantasy.

I like the alliteration of "shades and shadows." I also like the reading it invites. Bishop is denoting a tendency toward closeted rebellion, rebellion kept in a secret compartment. (She had wonderful manners, when sober.) The phrase connotes *sfumato,* however, the blurring of borderlines da Vinci learned from Verrocchio. (As a visual artist, Bishop preferred watercolor: a messy medium.) It connotes "negative capability," Keats's phrase for "being in uncertainties, mysteries, doubts, without any irritable reaching after fact and reason"—a capability ("nobody knows") Bishop did, in fact, appreciate.[23] It connotes abjection as well, or rather the transvaluation thereof. According to Kristeva, it isn't lack of cleanliness that causes abjection but what disturbs "identity, system, order," what disrespects "borders, positions, rules" (*Powers of Horror,* 4). For Bishop, it's an "awful" disturbance or disrespect—"yet cheerful," a Nietzschean turn enabled not only by the joy of writing but also by both renaissance painting and romantic poetry, both da Vinci and Keats.[24]

Why isolate the writer's desk? Why restrict myself to a study of that single piece of furniture, as opposed to the study containing it?[25] Structurally speaking, the desk is the stabilizing center of such a workroom. (Stephen King disagrees. "It starts with this," he crows: "Put your desk in the corner, and every time you sit

---

23. See *One Art,* 371–72 (to Lowell): "During the ten weeks I read & read & read—the 3-volume life of Byron, Greville in 3 volumes, Lucan (didn't you say you were reading that, too?), etc. etc.—and now am finishing the new edition of Keats's letters—all to what purpose I'm not sure, but all fascinating. At the moment I find the Keats the best of the lot, though. Except for his unpleasant insistence on the *palate,* he strikes me as almost everything a poet should have been in his day" (emphasis original).

24. See Goldensohn, 127–28.

25. For a critical look at Freud's study, see Sanders and Fuss. For a poetic one, see Cramer.

down there to write, remind yourself why it isn't in the middle of the room. Life isn't a support-system for art. It's the other way around" [101].) Rhetorically speaking, it's a synecdoche (or metonymy): The writer's desk—unlike, say, her bookcase—best represents the room of which it happens to be a part, much as that (slightly) disheveled pile of manuscripts best represents that (somewhat) unfamiliar desk.[26] Writers themselves—including Bishop, to judge from "12 O'Clock News"—tend to see it that way too. In fact, just about the only time they don't is when the study becomes too confining to work in, too confining to alleviate the anxiety of idleness: too organized, that is, or disorganized, or simply too familiar *(heimlich)*. (Benjamin warns himself not to write conclusions in "familiar" studies: "You would not find the necessary courage there" ["One-Way Street," 459].) When that happens, the figurative—or imaginary—potential of the desk seems to disappear. As Bishop told Merrill late in life and rather hyperbolically, "I've rarely written anything of value at the desk or in the room where I was supposed to be doing it—it's always in someone else's house, or in a bar, or standing up in the kitchen in the middle of the night" (quoted in Millier, 544).[27] (This, to me, indicates the play involved far more than the work. At any rate, notice her failure to mention writing in bed.)[28] Or as Bishop told the *Christian Science Monitor,* without hyperbole:

> Well, you get a place all set up. You have your books and pencils
> and papers ready. Then you find yourself writing some of your
> best lines standing up in the kitchen putting them on the back of
> an old envelope. This happened to me over and over. Inspiration
> isn't restricted to just one quiet room. (Quoted in Monteiro, 104)

Messy as she was, and notwithstanding any suggestion here to the contrary ("You have your books and pencils and papers ready"), it must have been overwhelming disorganization, not organization,

26. See Monteiro, 137: Bishop's best books "were on a [revolving] bookcase placed right next to her desk."

27. Moore "used a clipboard with the poem under construction on it" when away from her own desk, Bishop recalls: "'Even when I'm dusting or washing the dishes, Elizabeth'" (Bishop, "Efforts of Affection," in *Collected Prose,* 138).

28. See "Same Place Twice" and "Movable Type" for further discussion of this distinction between desk-bound work and desk-free play.

that Bishop found "awfully" confining at times.[29] And if not awfully confining, or anxiety producing, awfully *distracting*. Because in reality, there's no such thing as a tidy mess. And because for Bishop, the joyful creation of art, like the joyful experience of it, requires "a self-forgetful, perfectly useless concentration" unlikely to have been facilitated by disarray extreme enough to demand attention (quoted in Stevenson, *Elizabeth Bishop*, 66).

There's the joy of writing, and then, when all is said and done, there's the imaginary joy of not writing. In "The End of March," as in "In Prison," Bishop dreams of being confined to a solitary little place—a seaside hut—without a desk. (According to Bachelard, "in most hut dreams we hope to live elsewhere, far from the overcrowded house, far from city cares" [31]. For Barthes, such dreams concern closure—"delight in the finite." They're also juvenile: "To enclose oneself and settle, such is the existential dream of childhood" [*Mythologies*, 65].)[30] Not surprisingly, Bishop's place is a mess. For C. K. Doreski, the poem "represents an idea of art as a ramshackle structure that in its clumsy, organic, and decaying obtuseness dispels the illusion of an alternative reality" (44). For Lorrie Goldensohn, the place "has many things about it that seem as unlivably 'dubious' as . . . the poet's desk in '12 O'Clock News'"; Bishop's final renunciation, moreover, "constitute[s] a denial of what the poet recognizes as dangerous solitude, possibly wrapped in alcoholic haze" (262). Unlike "In Prison," however, there's to be no handwriting on the wall. The "hut dream" of "The End of March" is of doing nothing but look out windows (with binoculars), read boring books, write useless notes, talk to herself, and—sandpiper-wise—see things nearby:

> I wanted to get as far as my proto-dream-house,
> my crypto-dream-house, that crooked box
> set up on pilings, shingled green,
> a sort of artichoke of a house, but greener
> (boiled with bicarbonate of soda?),
> protected from spring tides by a palisade
> of—are they railroad ties?

---

29. See Travisano, 17–51, on Bishop and confinement.
30. See Bachelard, 29–37, more generally, on "the significance of the hut."

(Many things about this place are dubious.)
I'd like to retire there and do *nothing,*
or nothing much, forever, in two bare rooms:
look through binoculars, read boring books,
old, long, long books, and write down useless notes,
talk to myself, and, foggy days,
watch the droplets slipping, heavy with light.
At night, a *grog à l'américaine.*
I'd blaze it with a kitchen match
and lovely diaphanous blue flame
would waver, doubled in the window.
There must be a stove; there *is* a chimney,
askew, but braced with wires,
and electricity, possibly
—at least, at the back another wire
limply leashes the whole affair
to something off behind the dunes.
A light to read by—perfect! But—impossible.
And that day the wind was much too cold
even to get that far,
and of course the house was boarded up. (179–80,
    emphasis original)

Of course it was. Bishop never did get to be alone at last—sitting in the study amid the clutter, standing in the kitchen—without also having to be a lonely, alienated, joyful, and somewhat groggy artist who agonized over literary creation. Or, joyless, over the lack thereof.

Lucky her? Perhaps. This does happen to be true—or true enough—for many great writers, whether poets or not. Auden—not exactly unproductive—worked in similar conditions for similar reasons. So did Whitman.[31] So did Iris Murdoch, who, unlike T. S. Eliot, recommended that writers welcome rather than fear "whatever is contingent, messy, boundless, infinitely particular" (Murdoch, 260). But it needn't be true. Take Philip Roth, a onetime slob who, contrary to chaos theory, now appears to be a writer

---

31. See Poirier, 20: The debris scattered about Whitman's room "isn't a mess at all, but a way of assembling things so that he can exert maximum control over them."

finding imaginative disorder within domestic order. "If turbulence remains one of Roth's dominant literary tones, 'Order in living' is now his credo," writes David Remnick (79).[32] Or take E. B. White, whom John Updike associates with the "tidy, minimalist school of desk decor" (quoted in Krementz, viii) and who himself claimed, "A girl pushing a carpet sweeper under my typewriter table has never annoyed me particularly, nor has it taken my mind off my work, unless the girl was unusually pretty or unusually clumsy" (quoted in Krementz, 30).

Lucky him. Lucky housekeeper—something that can also be said, if not of Madeleine Chapelle, then of Céleste Albaret, the woman who enjoyed cleaning up after Proust.

---

32. Roth "lives like he's at Fort Dix," according to one current friend: "Everything precise and hospital corners" (quoted in Remnick, 79).

BEDTIME STORY

I do wish you could get up and exercise your little limbs from time to time. I *know* you have pain, etc.—but you are too valuable to take to your bed like a character in Proust.

—*Bishop (to Loren MacIver)*, One Art

MARCEL PROUST DIDN'T USE A DESK to write *À la recherche du temps perdu.* He used a bed. Or rather, he used one to continue writing. Proust never completed the enormous novel many readers—and translators—also fail to finish. Including Bishop, no doubt, with her recumbent "character." So why work there? And why not put the book itself to bed?

But before I consider these questions: what about those readers and translators? Jean Cocteau once wondered whether "'Proustians' read line by line or skip" (249). André Gide, of course, was one such Proustian when he skimmed the first few pages of *À la recherche* and decided not to publish it. (According to Albaret, Gide never opened the package.) But he was another kind of Proustian after his change of heart: the kind that can't finish the novel. So was Virginia Woolf—another writer I like a lot—and it's

19

instructive to compare the two.[1] Their analogous failures suggest the extent to which we should look beyond literary misreadings toward nonreadings—supplementing Harold Bloom's notion of the anxiety of influence not only with a Bishop-based concept of the anxiety of idleness but with a Barthesian concept of the fantasy of influence as well. (I'm referring here to Barthes's somewhat spurious admission: "And if I hadn't read Hegel, or *La Princesse de Clèves*...?—The book which I haven't read and which is frequently *told to me* even before I have time to read it (which is perhaps the reason I don't read it): this book exists to the same degree as the other: it has its intelligibility, its memorability, its mode of action" [*Roland Barthes by Roland Barthes*, 100, emphasis original].)[2] The failures suggest, in other words, that Proustian writers—if not Proustian readers—who to a certain extent merely imagine Proust feel both constrained and liberated. (I will not be so bold—so Proustian—as to delineate the limits of that liberation.) And they suggest ways in which any writer can afford to be "indifferent to [his or her] own stupidity." (Barthes adds, "Not to have read Hegel would be an exorbitant defect for a philosophy teacher, for a Marxist intellectual, for a Bataille specialist. But for me? Where do my reading duties begin? [The writer] agrees cheerfully enough to diminish or to divert the acuity, the responsibility of his ideas: in writing there would be the pleasure of a certain inertia, a certain mental *facility:* as if I were more indifferent to my own stupidity when I write than when I speak" [*Roland Barthes,* 100, emphasis original].) Or if not indifferent to her stupidity, to her ignorance.[3]

---

1. See Mares, 186: Woolf's comments on Proust reveal that her reading was "sporadic, selective, protracted, and in all likelihood, incomplete."

2. See Delany, 176: "I've always felt that the stories we tell ourselves about the books which we only know slightly and fleetingly, by rumor or inflationary report, end up being even more 'influential' than the works we encounter full on, absorb, judge, and come to occupy some balanced relation with. From well-read books we absorb the unquestioned laws of genre, the readerly familiarity with rhetorical figures, narrational tropes, conventional attitudes and expectations. From the others, however, we manufacture the dreams of possibility, of variation, of what might be done outside and beyond the genre that the others have already made a part of our readerly language."

3. See Ronell, 14: Barthesian stupidity is "the core recalcitration against which any writing breaks open."

By comparing Gide and Woolf, I mean, of course, to deconstruct any difference between their presumably analogous failures. Gide was annoyed—and impeded—by grammatical and syntactical errors in Proust; Woolf wasn't. He was impeded by a conceptual disagreement concerning homosexuality, thinking Proust should have written about pederasty instead of inversion; she wasn't. He found Proust insincere, "camouflaging" the author's homosexuality with the narrator's heterosexuality (*Journals of André Gide*, 2:276); she didn't. Yet Gide loved the novel, as did Woolf, hesitating and eventually failing to finish it in order to sustain the enjoyment it affords. The subordination of component parts to the whole, he wrote in "Apropos of Marcel Proust," is so deeply hidden that each page seems to find its perfect end in itself: "Hence this extreme slowness, this reluctance to quicken the pace, this continuous satisfaction" (in *Incidences*, 47).

Gide's remark in "Apropos of Marcel Proust" is a public affirmation. He was censorious in private, writing in his journal that the component parts are insubordinate, the attention to detail overwhelming:

Finished also *Les Jeunes Filles en fleurs* (which I notice that I had never read completely) with an uncertain mixture of admiration and irritation. Though a few sentences (and, in spots, very numerous ones) are insufferably badly written, Proust always says precisely what he wants to say. And it is because he succeeds so well in doing so that he delights in it. So much subtlety is, at times, utterly useless; he merely yields to a finicky need of analysis. But often that analysis leads him to extraordinary discoveries. Then I read him with rapture. I even like the fact that the point of his scalpel attacks everything that offers itself to his mind, to his memory; to everything and to anything whatever. If there is waste here, it's just too bad! What matters is not so much the result of the analysis as the method. Often one follows attentively, not so much the matter on which he is operating, as the minute work of the instrument and the slow patience of his operation. But it constantly appears to me that if the true work of art cannot do without that preliminary operation, it really begins only with that accomplished. The work of art presupposes it, to be sure, but rises up only after that original operation has ended. The architecture in Proust is very beautiful; but it often happens, since he removes none of the scaffolding, that the latter assumes more importance than the monument itself, in which one's glance, constantly distracted by the detail, does not succeed in grasping the whole. Proust knew this, and this is what made him, in his letters and in his conversation, insist so much on the general composition of his work: he was well aware that it would not be obvious. (3:404–5)

Woolf, on the other hand, was censorious in public, affirmative in private. Her essay "Phases of Fiction" complains about the attention to detail. Much of the difficulty of reading Proust, she writes, comes from this "content obliquity." In Proust, that is, the accumulation of objects that surround any central point is so vast and the objects themselves so remote, so difficult of approach and of apprehension, that this drawing-together process is "gradual, tortuous, and the final relation difficult in the extreme." There is so much more to think about than one had supposed, because "one's relations are not only with another person but with the weather, food, clothes, smells, with art and religion and science and history and a thousand other influences" (24). An early draft of the essay, however, justifies the attention. The long digressions, the disregard of time, and the enormous elaboration of analysis, Woolf writes, represent "the natural and right way of telling this particular story" (31). Should I even bother to interrogate this public-versus-private opposition? Perhaps, if only to trouble a somewhat spurious distinction to which many of us are attracted: the distinction between Gide the closet classicist, or formalist, and Woolf the closet romantic.

At any rate, all such distinctions between the French author and the British one collapse under the sign of incapacity. Both Gide and Woolf resisted reading—and finishing—Proust because he made it hard for them to write. (He makes it hard for everyone. "Proust's style had permeated my mind and changed my literary taste," writes Woolf biographer Phyllis Rose in *The Year of Reading Proust*. "A mixed blessing: everything I'd written before, whose chief virtues were clarity and brevity, now seemed pinched and parsimonious" [29].)[4] Woolf said so in letters and journals:

May 6, 1922, to Roger Fry:

Proust so titillates my own desire for expression that I can hardly set out the sentence. Oh if I could write like that! I cry. And at the moment such is the astonishing vibration and saturation and intensification that he procures—there's something sexual in it—that I feel I *can* write like that, and seize my pen, and then I *can't* write like that. (*Letters of Virginia Woolf,* 2:1244, emphasis original)

November 18, 1924:

No doubt Proust could say what I mean—that great writer whom I cannot read when I'm correcting, so persuasive is he. (*Diary of Virginia Woolf,* 2:322)

April 8, 1925:

I wonder if this time [with *Mrs. Dalloway*] I have achieved something? Well, nothing anyhow compared with Proust, in whom I am embedded now. The thing about Proust is his combination of the utmost sensibility with the utmost tenacity. He searches out these butterfly shades to the last grain. He is as tough as catgut & as evanescent as a butterfly's bloom. And he will I suppose both influence me & make me out of temper with every sentence of my own. (*Diary,* 3:7)

Gide said so both publicly and privately. "Each time I plunge anew into this lake of delights," he wrote in "Apropos of Marcel Proust," "I sit for days without daring to take up my own pen again, unable to admit—as is customary during the time that we remain under the spell of a masterpiece—that there are other ways of writing well, and seeing in what is called the 'purity' of my style

---

4. See Barthes, "From Work to Text," 163 (emphasis original): "I can delight in reading and re-reading Proust, Flaubert, Balzac [but] I also know that I cannot *re-write* them (that it is impossible today to write 'like that') and this knowledge, depressing enough, suffices to cut one off from the production of these works, in the very moment their remoteness established my modernity."

nothing but poverty" (in *Incidences,* 45). The *Journals,* however, are less self-aggrandizing and even manage to hit the nail on the head—or to hit the right note. Having heard a Mlle X. "dash off with extraordinary assurance and charm, to perfection," a number of pieces by Chabrier, Debussy, and Chopin, Gide confessed that he didn't dare "to open my piano for twelve days":

> Small wonder after that that I don't like pianists! All the plea-sure they give me is nothing compared to the pleasure I give myself when I play; but when I hear them I become ashamed of my playing—and certainly quite wrongly. But it is just the same when I read Proust; I hate virtuosity, but it always impresses me, and in order to scorn it I should first like to be capable of it; I should like to be sure of not being the fox of the fable. I *know* and *feel* for instance that Chopin's *Barcarolle* is to be played much more slowly than Mlle X. does, than they all do—but in order to dare to play it in the presence of others as *leisurely* as I like it, I should have to know that I could just as well play it much more rapidly and especially feel that whoever hears me is convinced of this. Played at that speed, Chopin's music becomes *brilliant,* loses its own value, its virtue. (2:265–66, emphasis original)

Sour grapes—or pianist envy.[5]

Woolf alone may have resisted finishing Proust because she felt engulfed by him—an eerie anticipation, as elsewhere in her oeuvre, of her own death by drowning. (Sink or swim. Gide, plunging into "this lake of delights," swam.) There had come a time, in 1934, when she felt time was running out. "So I came back and read Proust," she wrote composer Ethel Smyth, "which is of course so magnificent that I can't write myself within its arc; that's true; for years I've put off finishing it; but now, thinking I may, and indeed so they say must die one of these years, I've returned, and let my own scribble do what it likes. Lord what a hopeless bad book *[The Years]* will be!" (*Letters,* 5:304). Yet the water imagery, and the tenor thereof (whatever it may be), kept

---

5. One reason I don't like Gide is that he pretended to be a great musician. Not surprisingly, he never really played for anyone. See Kopelson, *Beethoven's Kiss,* 7–35.

holding her back: *eros* versus *thanatos* ("there's something sexual in it"), or maybe the other way around.

January 21, 1922, to E. M. Forster:

Everyone is reading Proust. I sit silent and hear their reports. It seems to be a tremendous experience, but I'm shivering on the brink, and waiting to be submerged with a horrid sort of notion that I shall go down and down and down and perhaps never come up again. (*Letters,* 2:1210)

June 20, 1928:

Take up Proust after dinner & put him down. This is the worst time of all. It makes me suicidal. (*Diary,* 3:186)

March 7, 1937, to Smyth:

And everyone seems chirping at me to read their damned works for them. And I want to sink into Proust. (*Letters,* 6:112)

Interestingly—or oddly—enough, it never seems to have occurred to either Gide or Woolf that they may have been too bored to finish, whatever boredom (or ennui) is. It certainly isn't an emotion in and of itself. Freud saw it as a form of anxiety. Barthes, in his autobiography, wonders whether boredom is his own form of hysteria. Patricia Meyer Spacks, in her literary history of boredom, describes ways in which it can mask rage, despair, irritation, alienation, frustration, emotional inadequacy, and either intellectual inferiority or intellectual superiority. She also distinguishes it from ennui: Whereas ennui implies a judgment of the universe, boredom implies a response to the immediate. Gide was too in touch with his irritation to be bored by Proust; Woolf too in touch with her sense of inferiority. The one who may have been bored is Barthes, who in *The Pleasure of the Text* both wonders whether anyone's ever read *À la recherche* word for word ("Proust's good fortune: from one reading to the next, we never skip the same passages" [11]) and includes a related passage with "Proust" written all over it.

> If I read this sentence, this story, or this word with pleasure, it is because they were written in pleasure (such pleasure does

not contradict the writer's complaints). But the opposite? Does writing in pleasure guarantee—guarantee me, the writer—my reader's pleasure? Not at all. I must seek out this reader (must "cruise" him) *without knowing where he is.* A site of bliss is then created. It is not the reader's "person" that is necessary to me, it is this site: the possibility of a dialectics of desire, of an *un-predictability* of bliss: the bets are not placed, there can still be a game.

I am offered a text. This text bores me. It might be said to *prattle.* The prattle of the text is merely that foam of language which forms by the effect of a simple need of writing. Here we are not dealing with perversion but with demand. The writer of this text employs an unweaned language: imperative, automatic, unaffectionate, a minor disaster of static (those milky phonemes which the remarkable Jesuit, van Ginnekin, posited between writing and language): these are the motions of ungratified suck-ing, of an undifferentiated orality, intersecting the orality which produces the pleasures of gastrosophy and of language. You address yourself to me so that I may read you, but I am nothing to you except this address; in your eyes, I am the substitute for nothing, for no figure (hardly that of the mother); for you I am neither a body nor even an object (and I couldn't care less: I am not the one whose soul demands recognition), but merely a field, a vessel for expansion. It can be said that after all you have writ-ten this text quite apart from bliss; and this prattling text is then a frigid text, as any demand is frigid until desire, until neurosis forms in it. (4–5, emphasis original)

To continue that Cocteau quotation: "I wonder if the 'Proustians' read line by line or skip. One is alarmed, physically speaking, for his apparently remarkable translators. The very idea of their task overwhelms us with fatigue" (249–50).[6] Barthes's friend Richard

---

6. No Proust translator has ever finished the entire novel. Of the English ones: C. K. Scott Moncrieff died after translating the first six parts, and the seventh part was translated by Stephen Hudson in England and Frederick Blossom in the United States; Andreas Mayor retranslated the seventh part and then died after beginning the remainder; Terence Kilmartin revised the Scott Moncrieff translation and then died after undertaking a second revision eventually done by D. J. Enright; James Grieve abandoned his translation after the Enright appeared.

Howard did abandon his complete translation for reasons related to fatigue. (Howard's English translations of numerous other works of French literature include ones of Barthes's.) Walter Benjamin, however, who undertook the first German version in collaboration with a friend, Franz Hessel, did not. Then again, he had only half the novel to do. (Howard and Benjamin are also writers I like a lot, the latter despite the fact that he doesn't really address—or "cruise"—anyone.)[7]

First of all, Benjamin became bored—bored insofar as, without quite realizing it, he felt intellectually superior. After years of what he considered prevarications by publishers, Benjamin was no longer inclined to return to the drudgery of the translation, particularly because his interests had shifted to other fields of literary production.[8] Before the shift of interests, however, Benjamin had found the coincidence of various interests disabling. When he read his lover, Asja Lacis, the lesbian scene involving Mlle Vinteuil and her nameless friend—Walter and Asja were in bed at the time, eating marzipan—she seemed to grasp its savage nihilism. She seemed to grasp, that is, how Proust ventures into the private chamber marked *sadism* and then smashes everything to bits, "so that nothing remains of the untarnished, clear-cut conception of wickedness, but instead within every fracture evil explicitly shows its true substance—'humanity,' or even 'kindness'" (*Moscow Diary,* 94). And when he put it to her that way, Benjamin did grasp how closely this coincided with the thrust of his own book on the baroque: "Proust was here developing a conception that corresponds at every point to what I myself have tried to subsume under the concept of allegory" (95). Tried to subsume, and probably failed. He'd also found the entire undertaking somewhat ridiculous. The critics may like his translation of *À l'ombre des*

---

7. See Harlow, 170: "Whereas Heidegger beckoned to his followers, Benjamin is prone rather to dismiss them, his a gesture of repudiation."
8. Proust himself, having spent years translating Ruskin in collaboration with Marie Nordlinger, might have sympathized. The *achevé d'imprimer* of *La Bible d'Amiens* was February 15, 1904, but, according to George Painter, it wasn't too late for Proust to add last-minute corrections: "In the small hours of that very day he sent two questionnaires to Mlle Nordlinger on passages which still perplexed him, ending with the ominous words: 'This old man'—meaning Ruskin—'is beginning to bore me'" (2:7).

jeunes filles en fleurs, he wrote Hugo von Hofmannsthal, but so what? Any such translation "has something *absurd* about it" (*Moscow Diary,* 135, emphasis original).

Second of all, Benjamin may have felt aesthetically inferior. Not only would he have written poetry if he could, but he suspected that translators should be poets as well—which Howard is, of course. Don't we, Benjamin asks in "The Task of the Translator," usually regard that which lies beyond communication in a literary work as "the unfathomable, the mysterious, or the 'poetic'?" And is this not something that a translator can reproduce "only if he is also a poet?" (70) (Stoppard concurs yet, in *The Invention of Love,* has Housman say that translation should be literal.) Even so, Benjamin did finalize a Baudelaire translation.[9]

Benjamin never finished his own (quotation-riddled) masterpiece either—a project inspired by the skylit shopping arcades of Paris—in part because it kept him from killing himself. It was, he felt, the actual, if not the only reason not to lose courage in the struggle for existence. The Parisian arcades inspired "The Task of the Translator" as well. A real translation is transparent, Benjamin writes. It doesn't cover the original, or block its light. This can be achieved, above all, by a literal rendering of the syntax, which proves words rather than sentences to be the primary element of the translator: "For if the sentence is the wall before the language of the original, literalness is the arcade" ("Task," 79). An unpoetic point of view, given that poetic translations aren't literal.

A third reason for Benjamin's failure may stem from Proust's attention to detail, even more overwhelming for a translator than for a reader. As one review describes—yet interrogates—the collaborators' division of labor: Whereas Benjamin represented Proust's exhaustive, intellectual side, Hessel represented his affectionate, intuitive one. Proust, however, isn't that parsable: "Almost every sentence of this gigantic work is a miracle of modulation and nuance." Nor, the reviewer adds, are these translators: "Hessel is sufficiently thoughtful, and Benjamin has shown not only here, but also in his Baudelaire translations, just what strong emotions

---

9. Cf. Brodersen, 117: Benjamin's estate contains numerous versions of poems from *Les Fleurs du mal,* only four of which were published in his lifetime.

and powers of expression he can summon to convey poetic virtues and resonances" (quoted in Brodersen, 169). A poetic viewpoint after all.

A more likely reason for the failure stems, not from Proustian detail, but from the linguistic dislocation most translators experience, even ones who also write poetry. Benjamin, in "The Task of the Translator," invokes nature to describe this alienation: "Unlike a work of literature, translation does not find itself in the center of the language forest but on the outside facing the wooded ridge; it calls into it without entering, aiming at that single spot where the echo is able to give, in its own language, the reverberation of the work in the alien one" (76). Banana Yoshimoto invokes it as well. "What would be an appropriate metaphor to explain my feelings when I was doing a translation?" asks the narrator of *N.P.,* her novel about suicidal translators.

> An endless meadow of golden pampas grass swaying in the wind, or a coral reef beneath a deep brilliant blue ocean. That utter stillness you feel when you're seeing a whole bunch of tropical fish swimming by, all in bright colors, and they don't even look like living creatures. (*N.P.,* 24)

"You're not going to live long with that kind of world in your head," she adds (24). But it is the unpoetic translator—the Benjamin, according to Benjamin—who is more likely to experience the dislocation. To quote another one of his metaphors: The enormous danger inherent in all translation is that "the gates of a language thus expanded and modified may slam shut and enclose the translator with silence" ("Task," 81).

A final reason for the failure is that Benjamin identified with Proust, notwithstanding any intellectual superiority or aesthetic inferiority. And as with both Gide and Woolf, this identification made it hard for him to write. The mother of Yoshimoto's narrator describes the problem—as well as the intense literary mediation of translation—in general terms. She feels that you become so involved with the writer's style it starts to feel like your own; that when you spend hours every day with that style, you end up thinking you alone created it in the first place; and that you get so far into the author's thought processes you sense no resistance at all. "Sometimes I find myself thinking the way she would," the mother admits, "not just about the book, but about my own life, even when I'm not translating" (118). Benjamin describes the problem in specific terms, admitting that his Proust translation necessitated "the *renunciation* of any dalliance with related possibilities" ("Berlin Chronicle," 5). But do related possibilities really exist, he wonders. They certainly permit no dalliance, because having begun to open the fan of memory, Proust never comes to the end of its segments. No one image ever satisfies him, for it too can be unfolded, and only in its folds does truth reside: that image, that taste, that touch for whose sake everything has been unfurled and dissected. "Such is the *deadly* game that Proust began so dilettantishly, in which he will hardly find more successors than he needed *companions*" (5–6, emphasis original). Benjamin also describes the problem in terms that anticipate—or predict—his own death, which he achieved by overdosing on morphine, just as Woolf describes it in terms that anticipate hers. The actual work, he wrote to his friend Gershom Scholem, made him sick. Unproductive involvement with a writer who so splendidly pursued goals that are similar to his own, at least former, goals "occasionally induces something like symptoms of internal poisoning in me" (*Correspondence of Walter Benjamin*, 305).

Howard was older than Benjamin when he undertook his translation. Benjamin had been thirty-four at the time; Howard was fifty-eight and therefore mature enough to come to believe that he might not live to complete it. At the beginning, he thought the work would take about a decade. He soon realized that it would take twenty years and that he'd do nothing else. He also appears to have been overwhelmed by the physical fatigue Cocteau mentions. "If I continued it would kill me," Howard told one reporter (Fritz Lanham). And so he limited himself to *Charlus,* a novel within the novel. Howard has indicated one reason for that maneuver: a suggestion by F. R. Leavis that *Daniel Deronda* contains a shorter, better novel about its (non-Jewish) heroine, Gwendolen Harleth. Of course, Edith Wharton had already extracted such a novel by writing *The House of Mirth.* One could credit Howard, I suppose. One could even attribute his decision to a preference for comedy. Charlus is, in fact, Proust's funniest character, although

Mme Verdurin gives him a run for his money. I myself, however, tend to credit motivations of which Howard appears unaware.

Before I indicate one such motivation, however, I should touch upon several other possible reasons. First of all, Howard wasn't bored. The complete translation, he told another reporter, involved pleasure very close to terror—a feeling that never abated because he was always within the clutches of something beyond his ability. That something, he explained, was the poetic attention to linguistic detail no novelist prior to Proust had paid, attention that conveys an impression of verbal immediacy, compensates for the formal incoherence of *À la recherche*, and accounts for the ten-year delay Howard anticipated. Yet another Proustian "incapacity." Yet another sense of aesthetic inferiority—even though Howard, unlike Benjamin, is a poet, which makes the sense somewhat false. Howard's brilliant translation of Proust's first sentence ("Time and again, I have gone to bed early" ["From *In Search of Lost Time*," 20]) shows him having risen to the challenge. (The novel both begins and ends on "Time," which no other English translator has sufficiently acknowledged.) He continued doing so. For example, whereas Proust's second sentence, in which the narrator remembers lying in the dark and drifting in between wakefulness and sleep, uses the phrase *"ma bougie éteinte"* (literally, "my candle extinguished"), both Terence Kilmartin and James Grieve drop the passive tone, the former saying "when I had put out my candle," and the latter, "as soon as I snuffed out my candle." Howard translated the phrase "my candle just out," which captures the vagueness of the original—the narrator's sense of not knowing whether he put out the candle himself or whether it flickered out of its own accord (quoted in Bernstein, 44).

Howard experienced linguistic dislocation as well, that feeling of finding himself outside Benjamin's language forest. "Every word has to be weighed in relation to what might be called the strangeness, the obliquity, the 'off' quality of Proust," he told another reporter (quoted in Bernstein, 74). (Woolf's "content obliquity" concerned detail, not dislocation.) Howard's own example, a passage in which Proust uses the peculiar expression *"cabinet de verdure"* to describe a room, echoes the sylvan image. "I couldn't find an easy reference for it," he said.

I thought it might mean a conservatory or a winter garden, but it doesn't. The existing translation translates it "arbor," and I wasn't sure about arbor. I called up friends in France and gradually it became clear that it was a place in the garden, what we might call a green nook, a secluded spot where the hedges were clipped in such a way as to make a kind of outdoor room. I don't think I was able to do much with this, but I wanted to know what it meant because I thought it would influence the tone. I think I translated it as a bower. (Quoted in Bernstein, 92)

Whereas Benjamin may have abandoned his translation because he identified with Proust, Howard may have done so because he disidentified. This I infer from "For James Boatwright, 1937–88," an elegy in *Like Most Revelations*:

> You went with a sigh of relief—to me a sign
> that any past we might hope to reclaim
> spreads like an oil slick, wide behind us,
> and the oncoming
>
> years of retrieval diminish even now
> until our name becomes, to memory,
> a synonym for weaknesses endured,
> or worse still, adored. (56)

Howard had planned to call *Le Temps retrouvé,* Proust's final volume, *Time Reclaimed.* Yet the poem implies that time can't be reclaimed, that our true past is irretrievable—even through involuntary memory, even through art. And so the poet himself may have disavowed the novelist's profound truth. He may feel that Proust's final point isn't one he need reach.

And yet Howard began his aborted translation at that point.[10] And yet a motivation I'm aware of—or which I imagine to be true—rests upon an identification with the "Marcel" who'd known Charlus, the Proust who hadn't yet discovered that truth. (I won't discuss his identification with the Charlus who'd known Marcel.)

---

10. Remembering Scott Moncrieff, who died before completing his translation, Howard began with the final volume before deciding to work from beginning to end. See Howard, "From *In Search of Lost Time*," 17.

For I believe that by pulling *Charlus* out of *À la recherche,* Howard has chosen, if only unconsciously, to translate the sections that concern, if not the one character who doesn't bore him, the one character with whom he associates Robert Phelps, a would-be older brother who, like Howard, also happened to have been gay and to have been from Ohio. The elegy "For Robert Phelps, Dead at 66" begins:

> *The Times* reports six years in Elyria,
>> browbeaten suburb of your childhood
> before my own had begun in Shaker Heights,
>> the brighter side of Cleveland's tracks . . .
> (40, ellipsis original)

But unlike Salinger, an only son who imagined Seymour Glass as the superior (male) sibling he never had, Howard is an only child who imagines Phelps as the inferior one. For Phelps *is* Charlus, for Howard. He's someone who should have been Proust, or Howard himself. (Kristeva hits this particular nail on the head: If Charlus had been less of a dilettante, she writes, he would have been Proust.)[11] To continue the poem:

> Granted: you would not write. Then your hand
>> began to shake so, you could not write. It was
>>> Parkinson's, as we would discover,
>
> but was it not at first a failure of your will?
>> Those years you passed off as "successes,"
>> triumphant manipulations of decor;
>>> I recall seasons when you devised
>
> "literaries"—a noun, *voyons*—for our latest
>> Mme Verdurin. Besides the fun,
> she paid far better than mere authorship, since
>> the rich, my dear, are always with us. (42)

Phelps was, moreover,

> the man I should be
>> if I had not been the child I was;

11. See Kristeva, *Time and Sense,* 95. All further Kristeva citations in this chapter are to *Time and Sense.*

> not son, not father either, but—I know it now—
> The lost brother found. *Vale frater.* (43)

Vale frater. Vale scriptor, if you'll forgive the less than florid Latin. I wonder whether either Benjamin or Howard would have had a different experience had Proust been alive when they were working on him. To translate a living author is to fall in love with him; it's an insinuation of self into otherness, according to George Steiner. And so to abandon that translation is to break things off too soon. But Proust was dead, and according to Nabokov, posthumous translation is disrespectful—a "profanation of the dead" (quoted in Steiner, 252). I disagree. I'd call any such translation mournful. The "hermeneutic motion" Steiner recommends—trust (an assumption that the original can be translated), penetration (an interpretative attack), embodiment (a dialectic in which the translation can be crippled), and restitution (an equilibrium between translation and original)—recalls the mourning process both Freud and Proust anatomize.[12] And so to abandon that translation is to fail to fully mourn. It is, in a sense, to remain melancholy.

Now, about that bed as well as that failure to finish writing. *À la recherche* is itself a translation. It's a translation, or mistranslation, of Proust's precursors: Corneille, Molière, Racine, even Scheherazade. (Bloom's idea.)[13] It's a translation of the prelinguistic thoughts these writers enabled Proust to have. (Benjamin's idea.)[14] And it's a translation of various writers Proust imitates. Proust, of course, was brilliant at pastiche. Here, for example, is how he begins doing Edmond and Jules Goncourt:

> The day before yesterday Verdurin drops in here to carry
> me off to dine with him—Verdurin, former critic of the *Revue,*
> author of that book on Whistler in which the workmanship, the
> painterly coloration, of the American eccentric is interpreted
> sometimes with great delicacy by the lover of all the refinements,

---

12. See Steiner, 312–19, 415–17.
13. For Steiner, "the 'abler soul' of the great precedent, the proximity of the rival version, the existence, at once burdensome and liberating, of a public tradition, releases the writer from the trap of solipsism" (484).
14. See Bolz and van Reijen, 27.

all the *prettinesses* of the painted canvas, that Verdurin is. And
while I am getting dressed to accompany him, he treats me
to a long narrative, almost at moments a timidly stammered
confession, about his renunciation of writing immediately after
his marriage to Fromentin's 'Madeleine,' a renunciation brought
about, he says, by his addiction to morphine and which had the
result, according to Verdurin, that most of the frequenters of his
wife's drawing-room did not even know that her husband had
ever been a writer and spoke to him of Charles Blanc, of Saint-
Victor, of Sainte-Beuve, of Burty, as individuals to whom they
considered him, Verdurin, altogether inferior. (*In Search of Lost
Time*, 6:27–29, emphasis original)

The morphine addiction to which Verdurin attributes this renunciation also anticipates Benjamin's death. And despite the prattle,
more naive than Proust's, one gets a good impression of the "liter-
aries" Howard's friend Phelps reproduced.

Because *À la recherche* is a translation as well, you may be
wondering whether Proust, like Howard, was simply too fatigued
to finish. But he wasn't. (According to Kristeva, Proust "never
tires of his continuous expansions" [303]. According to Benjamin,
finished works weigh less than those fragments on which great
writers work throughout their lives. Whereas the more feeble and
distracted take an inimitable pleasure in closure, feeling that their
lives have thereby been given back to them, "for the genius each
caesura, and the heavy blows of fate, fall like gentle sleep itself
into his workshop labor" ["One-Way Street," 446].) I myself, notwithstanding my sustained interest in the novel and knowledge of
Proust's work habits, have wondered whether he was too bored to
finish. But he couldn't have been. One writes to avoid boredom.
One writes, in part, to amuse oneself.[15] But if writing is a pleasure,
it's a painful one that justifies—or compensates for—the asocial
extremes to which it can lead and to which it certainly led Proust.
(Recall Barthes's claim that textual pleasure "does not contradict

---

15. Proust claims that the joy of both involuntary memory and art guarantees the
truthfulness of the past they do reclaim. Barthes implies that *À la recherche* was
"written in pleasure" (*Pleasure of the Text*, 4). Joseph Litvak calls the novel an "immense and intricate technology for the avoidance of boredom" (83).

the writer's complaints" [*Pleasures of the Text*, 4].) To quote Benjamin, Proust's radical attempt at self-absorption has as its center a loneliness that pulls the world down into its vortex with the force of a maelstrom: "And the overloud and inconceivably hollow chatter which comes roaring out of Proust's novels is the sound of society plunging down into the abyss of this loneliness." This, Benjamin believed, is the site of Proust's invectives against friendship. (So much for that affectionate side.)

> It was a matter of perceiving the silence at the bottom of this crater, whose eyes are the quietest and most absorbing. Something that is manifested irritatingly and capriciously in so many anecdotes is the combination of an unparalleled intensity of conversation with an unsurpassable aloofness from his partner. There has never been anyone else with Proust's ability to show us things; Proust's pointing finger is unequaled. But there is another gesture in amicable togetherness, in conversation: physical contact. To no one is this gesture more alien than to Proust. ("Image of Proust," 212)

Benjamin himself couldn't avoid that abyss, which may be the main reason why he positioned Proust's loneliness as central.

The "inconceivably hollow chatter" that comes roaring out of Proust. Wayne Koestenbaum, in "Logorrhea," has written about people who "chatter" and writers who prattle: "graphomaniacs" like the Goncourts and like Proust himself. Unlike the Goncourts, however, "Proust staves off the malodorous aura of logorrhea through his elegant symphonic paragraphing: each paragraph, a sculpted boundaried organism, develops a theme, a scene, a figure, and thus, though it is fueled by logorrhea, and is buoyed by an informing logorrheic tide, avoids the appearance of lost control, lost will" (105). But Proust can't stave off Benjamin's sense, our sense, of his loneliness. Although Barthes correctly described logorrhea as the piling up of words for the pleasure of it, the condition is always "a matter of solitary binge, of isolation" (Koestenbaum, 103).[16]

---

16. In "The Writer on Holiday," Barthes is quite sarcastic about the myth of Gide's logorrhea: "It is quite 'natural' that the writer should write all the time and in all situations. First, this treats literary production as a sort of involuntary secretion, which is taboo, since it escapes human determinations; to speak more decorously,

Nor can he stave off other negative aspects: logorrhea as a failure to be masculine, as an anti-Semitic slur, as an upper-class affliction. Then again, Proust couldn't have been epigrammatic, because logorrhea—"writing *against* the aphorism"—is an essential trait of memory writing (103, emphasis original). We need logorrhea, Koestenbaum writes, to retrieve the past: In a novel like Proust's, nostalgia takes the form of linguistic excess, imitating the loop of memory, and of "the distance of voice from the beloved objects it strives to recapture" (106).

Do prattlers address anyone? Does Proust—lonely Proust—converse? (Or cruise? Or ever play for anyone?) That depends upon the reader. Koestenbaum thinks not: "The malaise is never interpersonal, never dialogic" (103). Barthes thinks not, or pretended not to for the sake of argument: "I am the substitute for nothing, for no figure (hardly that of the mother)" (*Pleasure of the Text*, 5). Even Proust thought not. The essential difference between a book and a friend is not their degree of wisdom, he wrote in a preface to one of his Ruskin translations, "but the manner in which we communicate with them—reading, contrary to conversation, consisting for each of us in receiving the communication of another thought, while we remain alone, that is to say, while continuing to enjoy the intellectual power we have in solitude, which conversation dissipates immediately" (*On Reading*, 31). Genette, however, thinks he does: Every reader "knows himself to be the implied—and anxiously awaited—narratee of this swirling narrative that, in order to exist in its own truth, undoubtedly needs, more than any other narrative does, to escape the closure of 'final message' and narrative completion" (261). I think so too, one of the things that keeps me interested. But unlike Barthes (or a certain fantasy of Barthes), I also think that every reader—including Gide and Woolf, despite their analogous failures to finish—knows him- or herself to be positioned as Proust's mother in her entirety, as opposed to her body or body parts alone. Just as translators want

---

the writer is the prey of an inner god who speaks at all times, without bothering, tyrant that he is, with the holidays of his medium. Writers are on holiday, but their Muse is awake, and gives birth nonstop. The second advantage of this logorrhea is that, thanks to its peremptory character, it is quite naturally regarded as the very essence of the writer" (in *Mythologies*, 30).

paternal authors to love them back, demanding what Barthes in a pseudo-Lacanian section of *A Lover's Discourse* calls "the impossible reply" ("I love you, too" said simultaneously), novelists want maternal readers to do so (102). If gay, men who've "failed to be masculine," they also want these readers to accept them. Isn't it the mother, Eve Sedgwick asks in *Epistemology of the Closet,* to whom both the coming-out testament and its continued refusal to come out are addressed? And isn't some such scene behind the force of Proust's profanation of the mother? "That that woman who lovingly and fearfully scrutinizes narrator and narrative *can't know* is both an analytic inference (she never acts as if she knows, and anyway how could she know?) and a blank imperative: she *mustn't* know" (Sedgwick, 248, emphasis original). Lacan, however, suggests that what any novelist, like any child, really wants on an unconscious level is for the maternal reader not to love him back, not to accept him, not to read him. He must want her to help him realize that she can't meet all his demands. He wants to desire someone else.

"I am the substitute for nothing, for no figure (hardly that of the mother)" (Barthes, *Pleasure of the Text,* 5). For some reason, Barthes never felt that way when he played the piano, an activity he analogized to reading. What does the body do, he once asked, when it enunciates musically? It speaks, it declaims, "it doubles its voice" ("Rasch," 305). But the Barthesian body doesn't really double its own voice in an attempt to express itself. It doubles the voice of the mother. The Barthesian body signifies its senseless, sensuous, and dismembered self by impersonating the one woman who ever sees it whole, the one woman who ever lets it see itself whole. Maybe reading—or reading prattlers like Proust— remained, for Barthes, far more passive, far more disengaged than he'd have had it be. Barthes does indicate a secret fondness for certain readerly texts—in bed.[17] (Then again, according to Proust in that Ruskin preface, every writer shares that fondness: "Even those

---

17. See Barthes, "Soirées de Paris," 55: "In bed, to the music of the *Nutcracker* (broadcast to illustrate the notion of 'musical fantasy'!), I read a little more of the latest Yves Navarre (better than the others) and *M/S* ('yeah, yeah'); but these seem like chores and as soon as some of my obligations are fulfilled I put them aside and turn with relief to Chateaubriand, the real book. Always this notion: Suppose the

writers who to their contemporaries appeared to be the most 'romantic' read scarcely anything but the classics" [*On Reading,* 61]. Once again, so much for the distinction between Gide the closet classicist and Woolf the closet romantic.) And maybe it would have been less passive—less consumptive, more productive—if, like Gide and Woolf, Barthes never bothered to finish.

I can't quite describe the incompletion of *À la recherche.* Is the novel too short, Proust having failed to say everything he had to say? Or is it too long, Proust having failed to prune it properly? Once again, that depends upon the reader. Readers who need logorrhea—bookish readers bored by life, lonely readers with time on their hands—may find it too short. Readers running out of time may find it too long. Or not. "For years I've put off finishing it," wrote Woolf, "but now, thinking I may, and indeed so they say must die one of these years, I've returned" (*Letters,* 5:304). In "Getting into Death," however, a story by Thomas Disch, Cassandra Millar (a bedridden, terminally ill writer) resolves to finish Proust before she dies but never does—partly because this Proustian character finds herself both "bored and ravished by this dullest and best of all books," partly because she doesn't want to die, and partly because reading it enables her to approximate an understanding of death she knows she'll never really attain (179). Midway through, the character thinks that death will be like Proust, that death is what people talk about when you leave the room: "Not oneself, not the vanished, pitiable Albertine, but *their* business and appetites" (191, emphasis original). More than midway through, she thinks what might have to be her final, affectionate word on the subject: that "death is a social experience; an exchange; not a relationship in itself, but the medium in which relationships may exist; not a friend nor a lover, but the room in which all friends and lovers meet" (206).

Proust himself, a sickly Scheherazade who, according to Benjamin, was constantly aware of death, most of all when he was

---

Moderns were wrong? What if they had no talent?" Stoppard shares this fondness when it comes to prose fiction: "If I feel like reading fiction I find I really don't want to read the newest fiction. I like to go back to rather well-trod paths, with some exceptions. I want to read for the first time books of a period which I've never read. I read for solace rather than for stimulation" (quoted in Gussow, 126).

writing, and who, according to Painter, had resolved to die when *À la recherche* was done, failed to finish it, in part, because he didn't want to die. And yet he did want to die. *Eros* versus *thanatos*. (Or the other way around.) To quote the biographer, Proust's desire to complete the novel counterbalanced longing for the moment when "his sins would be instantaneously atoned and his mother's love eternally regained" (Painter, 2:326). He also longed not to suffer, either emotionally or physically. Cocteau alone, according to Benjamin, recognized what really should have been the major concern of all Proust readers: "He recognized Proust's blind, senseless, frenzied quest for happiness" (Benjamin, "Image of Proust," 203). And Benjamin alone recognized that Proust's terrible asthma was part of his art. Proust's syntax, Benjamin felt, rhythmically reproduced his fear of suffocating. His ironic, philosophical, and didactic reflections are the deep breath with which he shakes off the weight of memories. "On a larger scale, however, the threatening, suffocating crisis was death" ("Image of Proust," 214).

Another reason for the incompletion is that Proust was obsessive. Obsessive compulsives—not neatniks—fail to finish anything because they're frustrated by incompatible desires. Proust's incompatible desires relate to his mother, whom he both loved and hated. Or so suggests Kristeva, who sees Albertine as both Proust and his mother and who situates Albertine's sapphic profanation of the mother within the context of an earlier profanation of the father. The narrator, taking responsibility for the sins of both Mlle Vinteuil and the friend who profaned Mlle Vinteuil's father, links these two to both Albertine and Vinteuil, whose death is transformed into a "murder" of the mother. And so "when Albertine, the narrator's alter ego, loves other women, is she taking revenge on her mother?" (77). Kristeva's rhetorical question is, of course, homophobic, but I'd rather not read her symptomatically, except to say that she also indicates a "questionable interest" in Proust's sadomasochism (248). Maybe Proust can't stop writing because he can't stop torturing himself—and us. Maybe Kristeva can't. Writing, after all, is a painful pleasure.

If Albertine is the narrator's alter ego, she's not the only one. But she's the only one who isn't either a creative artist or a failed writer. Vinteuil, a composer, and Elstir, a painter, are two such artists. The Goncourts, who prattle without taking paragraph breaks, are two such writers. The drug-addicted Verdurin, who renounced writing, is another. The sickly Bergotte, who did nothing for almost twenty years and then died thinking that his novels paled in comparison with a painting by Vermeer, is another. ("I ought to have gone over them with a few layers of color, made my language precious in itself, like this little patch of yellow wall" [Proust, *In Search of Lost Time,* 5:244].) So is Charlus, who, according to Kristeva, would have been Proust if he, Charlus, had been less of a dilettante. So is Swann, who never finishes his essay on Vermeer. To continue quoting Kristeva: Whereas Proust surrounds Swann with irony as well as with a despondent, admiring affection, which we see in his visits to Combray, in his gardens, his Giotto prints, his Jewish mother, his licentious wife, and his pitiful death, Swann "reminds Proust of what might happen if he should ever stop writing" (34). But I wonder if Proust was aware of these identifications, including the one with Swann.[18] Or so I'm led to wonder by *The End of the Story,* a novel by Lydia Davis. Davis— yet another Proust translator (she did *Du côté de chez Swann*)—has her narrator, a translator writing about a failed love affair, admit,

> Then again, maybe there is nothing that does not belong in, and this novel is like a puzzle with a difficult solution. If I were clever and patient enough, I could find it. When I do a difficult crossword, I never quite finish it, but I usually don't remember to look at the solution when it appears. I have been working on this puzzle so long by now that I catch myself thinking it is time to look at the solution, as though I will only have to dig through

---

18. The only artist with whom the author of *À la recherche* may have identified on a conscious level is Vinteuil, who dies before transcribing his musical masterpiece— painstaking work eventually done by his daughter's friend. As such, Tadié considers the composer "allegorical" (762). (Like Proust, Vinteuil is a neatnik who leaves messy manuscripts for other people to organize: Vinteuil has "very strict views on 'the deplorable slovenliness of young people'" [Proust, *In Search of Lost Time,* 1:155], and "As in the illegible notebooks in which a chemist of genius, who does not know that death is at hand, jots down discoveries which will perhaps remain forever unknown, Mlle Vinteuil's friend had disentangled, from papers more illegible than strips of papyrus dotted with a cuneiform script, the formula, eternally true and forever fertile, of this unknown joy, the mystic hope of the crimson Angel of the Dawn" [5:349–50].)

a pile of papers to find it. I have the same sort of frustration, at times, with a problem in a translation. I ask, Now, what *is* the answer?—as though it existed somewhere. Maybe the answer is what will occur to me later, when I look back.

Because of the kind of puzzle this is, though, no one else will ever know that a few more things belonged in the novel and were left out because I did not know where to put them.

This is not the only thing I'm afraid of. I'm afraid I may realize after the novel is finished that what actually made me want to write it was something different, and that it should have taken a different direction. But by then I will not be able to go back and change it, so the novel will remain what it is and the other novel, the one that should have been written, will never be written. (87, emphasis original)

Proust, that is, might have realized these identifications had he not died writing the novel, had he been able to "look back" and discover such a solution. In fact, the only failed writer with whom Proust did realize he identified is a character in another novel by George Eliot: not Gwendolen Harleth in *Daniel Deronda,* but Edward Casaubon in *Middlemarch.*[19] But that was in 1899—long before he began *À la recherche.*

I've also wondered, for personal reasons, whether Proust was aware of having left his brother Robert out. Maybe this omission (repression) was inadvertent (unconscious), and Proust could have finished the novel had he corrected it—or simply "known where to put him." Genette calls this kind of omission *paralipsis* (the absence of one of the constituent elements of a situation in a period the narrative generally covers) and cited as an example "the fact of recounting his childhood while systematically concealing the existence of one of the members of his family (which Proust would be doing

---

19. For a further explanation of the identification with this unhappy character, see Eliot, 271: "For my part I am very sorry for him," writes the narrator of *Middlemarch.* "It is an uneasy lot at best, to be what we call highly taught and yet not to enjoy: to be present at this great spectacle of life and never to be liberated from a small hungry shivering self—never to be fully possessed by the glory we behold, never to have our consciousness rapturously transformed into the vividness of a thought, the ardor of a passion, the energy of an action, but always to be scholarly and uninspired, ambitious and timid, scrupulous and dim-sighted."

vis-à-vis his brother Robert if we took the *Recherche* for a genuine autobiography)" (51–52). After all, the narrator of *Jean Santeuil,* Proust's first novel, hasn't got a brother either, and that abandoned book is even closer to autobiography than *À la recherche.* But the narrator of *Contre Sainte-Beuve,* his second novel, does: a brother named Robert, and whose inclusion, moreover, didn't prevent the author from abandoning that book as well. And so the omission of the character in *À la recherche,* which synthesizes—or subsumes—the two previous books, was quite deliberate.[20]

What about the brothers Proust does include? How should we construe Basin de Guermantes and Palamède de Charlus, both uncles of Saint-Loup (the narrator's only friend, and the only character who ever touches him); Edmond and Jules Goncourt; Arnulphe and Victurnien de Surgis? I've nothing to say about the beautiful but idiotic Surgises, with whom, through Charlus, Proust must have disidentified.[21] Nor have I anything to say about the Goncourts, whom Proust presents as both naive and indistinguishable. Basin and Palamède ("Mémé"), however, feel for one another an intermittent affection they find hard to express, a nostalgic affection compromised by maternal knowledge that the senior, straighter sibling, to cite Sedgwick, mustn't possess.[22] To quote the scene that occurs shortly after Charlus cruises the Surgises:

> To return to this first evening at the Princesse de Guermantes's, I went to bid her good night, for her cousins, who had promised to take me home, were in a hurry to be gone. M. de Guermantes wished, however, to say good-bye to his brother, Mme de Surgis having found time to mention to the Duke as she left that M. de Charlus had been charming to her and to her sons. This great kindness on his brother's part, the first moreover that he had

---

20. See Tadié, 40 for various reasons why Robert "disappeared from the drafts of 'Combray.'"

21. See Nietzsche, 81: "What is it we long for at the sight of beauty? To be beautiful ourself: we imagine we would be very happy if we were beautiful.—But that is an error."

22. See Ladenson, 121–22: "*Mémé* is the familiar name by which bourgeois French children traditionally call their grandmothers. Proust's narrator would seem to be an exception to this practice, which is what allows Charlus's nickname to pass without comment."

ever shown in that line, touched Basin deeply and aroused in him old family feelings which were never dormant for long. As we were saying good-bye to the Princess he insisted, without actually thanking M. de Charlus, on expressing his fondness for him, either because he genuinely had difficulty in containing it or in order that the Baron might remember that actions of the sort he had performed that evening did not escape the eyes of a brother, just as, with the object of creating salutary associations of memory for the future, we give a lump of sugar to a dog that has done its trick. "Well, little brother!" said the Duke, stopping M. de Charlus and taking him tenderly by the arm, "so we walk past our elders without so much as a word? I never see you now, Mémé, and you can't think how I miss you. I was turning over some old letters the other day and came upon some from poor Mamma, which are all so full of tenderness for you."

"Thank you, Basin," M. de Charlus replied in a broken voice, for he could never speak of their mother without emotion.

"You must let me fix up a cottage for you at Guermantes," the Duke went on.

"It's nice to see the two brothers being so affectionate towards each other," the Princess said to Oriane.

"Yes, indeed! I don't suppose you could find many brothers like them. I shall invite you with him," the Duchess promised me. "You've not quarreled with him? . . . But what can they be talking about?" she added in an anxious tone, for she could catch only an occasional word of what they were saying. She had always felt a certain jealousy of the pleasure that M. de Guermantes found in talking to his brother of a past from which he was inclined to keep his wife shut out. She felt that, when they were happily together like this and she, unable to restrain her impatient curiosity, came and joined them, her arrival was not well received. But this evening, this habitual jealousy was reinforced by another. For if Mme de Surgis had told M. de Guermantes how kind his brother had been to her so that the Duke might thank his brother, at the same time certain devoted female friends had felt it their duty to warn the Duchess that her husband's mistress had been seen in close conversation with his brother. And Mme de Guermantes was tormented by this. . . .

"Come along, Basin; good night, Palamède," said the
Duchess, who, devoured by rage and curiosity, could endure
no more. "If you have made up your minds to spend the night
here, we might just as well stay to supper. You've been keeping
Marie and me standing for the last half-hour." The Duke parted
from his brother after a meaningful hug, and the three of us
began to descend the immense staircase of the Princess's house.
(*In Search of Lost Time,* 4:157–61, first ellipsis original)

"For the genius each caesura, and the heavy blows of fate, fall
like gentle sleep itself into his workshop labor," writes Benjamin
("One-Way Street," 446). Of course, the fundamental reason
Proust never finished *À la recherche* is that this genius labored
where most writers only read, sleep, seduce, make love, or simply
masturbate. (And in Benjamin's case, eat marzipan.) In addition
to the pleasure afforded by the project, or to the pleasurable pain;
in addition to the logorrhea, or the obsession, to which the author,
while prone, was prone; in addition to the unfortunate likelihood
that he'd die upon completion; in addition to any problematic
paralipsis—Proust, almost always bedridden (unlike Bishop, an
asthma sufferer sufficiently medicated to move around), simply
needed something interesting to keep doing there. (In reality,
Gide wrote standing up at a desk; in fantasy, sitting down in public and without a desk. Woolf really wrote in private rooms—and
huts—of her own: as a youth standing at a drafting table, to emu-
late her older sister, as an adult sitting at a desk. Benjamin, a political refugee, worked at desks in foreign libraries. Howard works
at a desk in his living room, surrounded—as Barthes would put
it—by an "exemplary library of reference books" [*Roland Barthes,*
159].)[23] And although Proust considered his bed a kind of boat, or
"shallop" (quoted in Painter, 2:295), what it really was is a kind of
nest. "I was thinking these thoughts and dreaming these dreams,"
writes Bachelard in concluding his chapter on nests, "when I read
a passage in the autumn 1954 issue of *Cahiers G.L.M.* that encour-
aged me to maintain the axiom that identifies the nest with the
world and makes it the center of the world."

---

23. See Gide, *Journals of André Gide,* 2:347–48: "I am apt to write in the train,
in the *métro,* on a bench along the quay or along the boulevards, on road embank-
ments, and those are my best pages, the most truly inspired."

Here Boris Pasternak speaks of "the instinct with the help of which, like the swallow, we construct the world—an enormous nest, an agglomerate of earth and sky, of death and life, and of the two sorts of time, one we can dispose of and one that is lacking." Yes, two sorts of time, for what a long time we should need before waves of tranquility, spreading out from the center of our intimacy, reached the ends of the world.

"What a concentration of images in Pasternak's swallow's nest!" reaffirms Bachelard. "And, in reality, why should we stop building and molding the world's clay about our own shelters? Mankind's nest, like his world, is never finished. And imagination helps us to continue it" (104, footnote omitted).[24]

Depending on the needs, habits, and proclivities of the occupant, nests can be either tidy or messy. (In reality, admits Bachelard, "few dreamers of nests like a swallow's nest which, they say, is made of saliva and mud" [102].) Proust's bed is exceptional, not to mention paradoxical. Unlike Bishop's desk, it really was a tidy mess. This achievement comports with Proust's needs—finding debris distracting, he liked things shipshape—if not with his slovenly work habits. It also comports with the style and structure of the work of art he created there, a tidy mess of a novel if ever there was one.[25] (Gide's least favorite messy detail: the faulty grammar; my favorite one: the dead people at the final reception. How do you forget you've killed someone?) But the organization was done

---

24. Cf. Adorno, 87: "Properly written texts are like spiders' webs: tight, concentric, transparent, well-spun, and firm. They draw into themselves all the creatures of the air. Metaphors flitting hastily through them become their nourishing prey. Subject matter comes winging towards them. The soundness of a conception can be judged by whether it causes one quotation to summon another. Where thought has opened up one cell of reality, it should, without violence by the subject, penetrate the next. It proves its relation to the object as soon as other objects crystalize around it. In the light that it casts on its chosen substance, others begin to glow." (One recalls Bishop: "A group of words, a phrase, may find its way into my head like something floating in the sea, and presently it attracts other things to it" [quoted in Monteiro, 25].)

25. For an unappreciative view of another such artwork (the film *Last Year at Marienbad*), see Kael, 188–89 (ellipsis and emphasis original): "Resnais: 'Make of it what you will . . . whatever you decide is right.' This is like making a mess and asking others to clean it up; it's also a cheap way of inviting audiences and critics to make fools of themselves. And they do: they come up with 'solutions' like *'Marienbad* is supposed to be interpreted like a Rorschach test—you are supposed

by Albaret, who in *Monsieur Proust* describes both Proust's fas-
tidiousness, which he must have gotten from his mother, and the
housework it entailed:

> As soon as he was gone I set to work on his room. As he never
> put anything away or picked anything up, the bed was always
> covered with papers and newspapers; pens and handkerchiefs
> lay around where they'd fallen or been thrown aside. I tidied the
> room and aired it and put some woolies on the chair in case he
> was cold or wanted to change when he came in. (119)[26]

He got the bed—his brass childhood bed—from mother as well.
The messy nest Albaret kept neat was the one in which Proust
himself had been, if not hatched, so memorably kissed goodnight.
(Needless to say, it was also the one in which he sickened and
died.) As such, it was a bit small for an adult and far too small for
two—a correlative of the author's extreme isolation, or of the creator's lonely existence. For fond of him as she was, and he of her, Albaret failed to become a true companion—unlike, say, "Baroness"
Marta, the maid who marries her employer in Chatwin's novel
Utz. These two, in Albaret's account, never exchange a "meaningful hug." They don't even touch.

Proust, of course, wasn't the first writer to work in bed. So did
Descartes, perhaps. So did Pushkin, who wasn't even sick at the
time. So did Heinrich Heine and Mark Twain, who were. Proust

---

to give it whatever meanings you wish.' But, but—a Rorschach test is a blot, an accident onto which you project your own problems and visions; it is the opposite of a
work of art, which brings the artist's vision to *you*. And *Marienbad*, though it's silly
albeit at times amusing and pretty, is in no way an *accidental* blot. And whatever
is there to decide *about*? A riddle that has no answer may seem deep if that's your
turn of mind or it may just seem silly and pointless. Did they meet before or didn't
they? It's rather like Which Twin Has the Toni. You have to work hard to pretend
it's a complicated metaphysical question. If you compose a riddle and then say all
solutions are right, then obviously there is no solution, and the interest must be in
the complexity or charm or entertainment of the riddle and the ideas or meanings it
suggests to you—in its *artfulness*. And at this level, *Marienbad* is a mess—or, rather,
it's a neat mess, and it's too heavy to be so lightweight."

26. This, to say the least, represents an unusual arrangement. Most female servants
at the time were told not to disturb the master's study. The sexist, elitist assumption
was that they couldn't fathom the organization of such a place. One presumes that
Bishop had servants stay away from her desk as well—yet another reason she was
bothered by the mess.

wasn't even the only modernist to do so: Anna de Noialles, for example, had her own nest at more or less the same time, as did Colette. (Anglo-Americans include Wharton and Joyce.) Nor am I suggesting a direct correspondence between literary form and *literary* form: Messy nesters aren't necessarily messy novelists, and tidy nesters, tidy novelists. (The same goes for painters: Whereas Mondrian's studio was as neat as his work, Francis Bacon produced uncluttered painting in a cluttered environment. Degas produced work neither tidy nor untidy in a messy studio no one ever organized.) I'm not even suggesting a correspondence between Proust's work habits and those of his literary alter egos, none of whom nested. Casaubon, in *Middlemarch*, was a desk-bound neatnik who cleaned up after himself. Swann, who "manifests a nostalgia for an erudite aesthetics in filling his apartment with bibelots," was a desk-bound collector who surrounded himself with inspirational objets d'art (Watson, 72). Proust was no *bibeloteur*—or rather he stopped being one after *Jean Santeuil*.[27] (Like Flaubert before him, the author of *À la recherche* had become relatively "indifferent to his surroundings" [Watson, 69].)[28] As for the literary alter egos with whom Proust clearly disidentified, the failed writers with whom his identifications, if any, were undoubtedly unconscious and hence whose writing habits, if any, should be read symptomatically: the Goncourts, like Swann, were *bibeloteurs;* we don't

27. See Watson, 148, 158, 166: *Jean Santeuil* indicates that "the relationship between persons and their furnishings has changed over the past fifty years," an "estrangement" in which "intimate, affective" connection to things disappeared. See also Tadié, 160: For Proust, "aestheticism degenerates into 'idolatry' when the artist decides to make a work of art out of his life and his surroundings."

28. Albaret, however, was relatively attentive. To cite, at length, her description of his bedroom: "To the left of the piano facing the windows was a massive oak desk piled with books. The wall to the left, still facing the windows, was the one with the mantelpiece, the candelabra, and the clock. In the right-hand wall were two tall double doors, one at each end, opening into the main salon. The one nearer the window was the usual entrance to the bedroom; it was covered by a curtain, and one half of the folding door was always kept shut. The other door was never used at all; in any case, it was blocked by two revolving bookcases, laden with volumes as was the oak table. Against the wall, to the left of the door that was used, there was a pretty little Chinese cabinet with photos on it of him and his brother as children. M. Proust kept his money and bank papers in the drawers of this cabinet; when he went out he usually asked me to get from it whatever he needed. Next to the little cabinet was a large rosewood chest matching the wardrobe. It had a white marble

know the habits of either Charlus or Verdurin; and while Bergotte retires from his study to his bedroom as an invalid, he does so only after he stops writing—indeed, only after he goes blind. At any rate, none of these men died writing interminable books.[29]

Or is it more accurate to say that Proust killed himself by writing the novel? Writers, according to Kristeva, aren't supposed to renounce *life*. (Many do, of course: Woolf, Benjamin, even Barthes in a way, who might have recovered from having been hit by that laundry truck. Kafka could have explained all such deaths. Despair is an enemy of both life and writing, he wrote, because writing is merely a moratorium—as it is for someone who makes a will just before hanging himself.) When Albertine commits suicide, the critic writes in yet another homophobic spasm, we see "the tyranny of remorse" in lesbians and the "criminal lunacy" of the character's obsession—a lunacy that enables the narrator to distance himself from the temptation of suicide and that clears a path toward art, that "substitute" for grief and remorse. "Succumbing neither to melancholy nor to flagellation but playing every possible role at the same time," he buries both Albertine and his illusions about love—maintaining thereby that the creator is inherently solitary (82). On the other hand, Kristeva acknowledges, writers do succumb to melancholy, especially ones who never stop. (Think of Bishop.) Death is not a final destination

---

top, on which there were two white bowls with scalloped edges, on either side of a white statuette of the Infant Jesus crowned with bunches of grapes. Above it was a big mirror reaching to the ceiling. Also on the chest were the thirty-two black imitation-leather notebooks containing the first draft of his book, which he always kept there. In the drawers were all sorts of photographs and souvenirs amassed in the course of the years" (Albaret, 55). As for the proximate work space: "He had everything he required beside him: next to the screen, the pretty little bamboo table laden with books and, on the left, a pile of handkerchiefs; then the night table with the doors open, holding the manuscripts he was working on, and in front of them a bunch of pen holders, one or two inkwells, and his watch. They were always ordinary little watches—I used to buy them for five francs each, I remember. He wouldn't have any others" (271). See Tadié, 448: "Unlike many people who are ill, Marcel did not like receiving presents or possessing objects (or even books), for the very good reason—he who had visited so many museum collections—that he did not like collecting things: everything was either in the mind or else in museums; happiness depended neither on other people, nor on objects."

29. See Watson, 66–69. See also *In Search of Lost Time,* 2:200, 3:443, 3:444, 3:447, 5:240.

but an indispensable part of life, its "constitutive intermittence" (313). In this sense, sadomasochism is the inevitable counterpart to the imaginary, hidden, and necessary face of delicacy. In this sense, Sade, too, was one of Proust's precursors. Think of Charlus, who is elegant because he is mad. Or think of the narrator, whose subtlety stems from having allowed—or caused—both Albertine and his grandmother to die. "Interminable remorse," writes Kristeva, is a formula for putting off indifference, "a way of delaying it in the name of style" (313).

Time and again, I have tried to write an entire book—to be titled *Finishing Proust*—about all this. If I ever succeed, I wonder what kind of book it will have been. Will it have been an elegy—either Proustian or Barthesian—for Steve, that second Seymour who wandered off to Israel over twenty years ago and then killed himself: one the completion of which enables me not to do so too? (Terminable remorse.) Will it have been a pseudo-elegy, at the end of which I do it anyway: a poor substitute for true remorse? (Terminal remorse.) On the other hand, who's to say I haven't finished *Finishing Proust*? And who's to say, who am I to say, Proust didn't finish *À la recherche du temps perdu*? Or that Benjamin and Howard didn't finish their translations, Gide and Woolf their readings? According to Blanchot—notwithstanding his competing notion of *désoeuvrement* (or "unworkable" idleness [13, 22]), which I'd attribute to the man's having been a Cocteau Proustian—a work of art is neither complete nor incomplete. It simply *is*.

SAME PLACE TWICE

The attractively disordered clutter of the presents from the faithful
which had followed the lady of the house from place to place and
had come in time to assume the fixity of a trait of character, of a line
of destiny; the profusion of cut flowers, of chocolate-boxes, which
here as in the country systematized their efflorescence in accordance
with an identical mode of blossoming; the curious interpolation of
those singular and superfluous objects which still appear to have just
been taken from the box in which they were offered and remain
forever what they were at first, New Year presents; all those things,
in short, which one could not have isolated from the rest but which
for Brichot, an old habitué of Verdurin festivities, had that patina,
that velvety bloom of things to which, giving them a sort of depth, a
spiritual *Doppelgänger* has come to be attached—all this sent echoing
round him so many scattered chords, as it were, awakening in his
heart cherished resemblances, confused reminiscences which, here in
this actual drawing room that was speckled with them, cut out, de-
fined, delimited—as on a fine day a shaft of sunlight cuts a section in
the atmosphere—the furniture and carpets, pursued, from a cushion
to a flower-stand, from a footstool to a lingering scent, from a lighting
arrangement to a color scheme, sculpted, evoked, spiritualized, called
to life, a form which was as it were the idealization, immanent in
each of their successive homes, of the Verdurin drawing-room.

—*Proust,* The Captive

I SEEM TO HAVE ACCUSED ROLAND BARTHES of a considerable amount
of pretense over the years. I've accused him of pretending to reveal
singular truths he really keeps to himself for fear readers might
believe them and hence jeopardize his unconventionality. I've also
accused him of three kinds of wishful thinking: pretending to be a
happier, less "Wertheresque" homosexual than he really was; pretending to be a happier, more optimistic critic than he really was
(unlike Benjamin, who pretended pessimism); and pretending (if
only to himself, unlike Gide) to be a better pianist than he really
was, or of "hallucinating perfection" at the keyboard.[1] I've now accused this intellectual author of pretending not to believe in authors

---

1. See Kopelson, "Wilde, Barthes, and the Orgasmics of Truth"; *Love's Litany,*
129–50; and *Beethoven's Kiss,* 7–33.

and not to see himself as intellectual—or at least of defining the intellectual in such a way as to preclude the predication. I've accused him of pretending Proust is nonconversational, presumably for the sake of argument. I've even accused him of pseudo-Lacanianism. Needless to say, all such accusations say more about me.[2]

Yet I believe Barthes when he describes "protocols" of writing.[3] I believe him, in part, because I can't imagine why he'd lie about work habits. I also believe him because the descriptions make sense—sense Barthes himself doesn't fully appreciate. They situate both desk and "text" as structural equivalents—more specifically, as homologous substitutions for Barthes's erotic body, itself a substitution (or alibi) for his basically egocentric but woefully unoriginal subjectivity.[4] Allow me to quote at considerable length. In a 1973 interview concerning a number of protocols, we first learn the stylistic importance of fountain pens:

> I would say, for example, that I have an almost obsessive relation to writing instruments. I often switch from one pen to another just for the pleasure of it. I try out new ones. I have far too many pens—I don't know what to do with all of them! And yet, as soon as I see a new one, I start craving it. I cannot keep myself from buying them.
>
> When felt-tipped pens first appeared in the stores, I bought a lot of them. (The fact that they were originally from Japan was not, I admit, displeasing to me.) Since then I've gotten tired of them, because the point flattens out too quickly. I've also used

2. See Kopelson, *Queer Afterlife of Vaslav Nijinsky,* 123: "Many people—gay or not, Freudian or not, Lacanian or not—associate identification with misrecognition and self-expression with misrepresentation. I, for one, insist that my own narcissism is merely performative, or theatrical, yet feel most myself when pretending to be less intelligent and attractive than I really am." Barthes is equally insistent. See, for example, *Camera Lucida,* where he uses egocentrism "heuristically" (8), reads himself "symptomatically" (18), and universalizes his particularity—"utopically" (72).

3. See Barthes, "An Almost Obsessive Relation to Writing Instruments," 178: "Personally, I call the set of those 'rules' (in the monastic sense of the word) which predetermine the work—and it is important to distinguish the different coordinates: working time, working space, and the action of writing itself—the 'protocols' of work. The etymology is clear: it means the first page glued to a manuscript in preparation for writing."

4. Nor is there anything original about calling Barthes a closet humanist. See Goldberg, 281–91, for an analogous reading. See also Burke. Cf. Smith, 108: Barthes sees subjectivity as "an infinite and infinitely mobile collection of subject-positions in cahoots with given discourses but never entirely given over to them."

pen nibs—not the "Sergeant-Major," which is too dry, but softer
nibs, like the "J." In short, I've tried everything . . . except Bics,
with which I feel absolutely no affinity. I would even say, a bit
nastily, that there is a "Bic style," which is really just for churn-
ing out copy, writing that merely transcribes thought.

In the end, I always return to fine fountain pens. The essential
thing is that they can produce that soft, smooth writing I absolutely
require. ("Almost Obsessive Relation," 178, ellipsis original)[5]

We then learn that Barthes isn't as technophobic as this pen obsession suggests.

In my case, there are two stages in the creative process. First
comes the moment when desire is invested in a graphic impulse,
producing a calligraphical object. Then there is the critical
moment when this object is prepared for the anonymous and
collective consumption of others through transformation into
a typographical object (at that moment, the object is already
beginning its commercialization). In other words—first I write
the text with a pen, then I type the whole thing on a typewriter
(with two fingers, because I don't know how to type).

Up until now, these two stages—handwriting, typewriting—
were, in a way, sacred for me. But I should note that I am trying
to change my ritual.

I have bought myself a present: an electric typewriter. Every
day I practice for half an hour, in the fond hope of acquiring a
more "typewriterly" writing. (179)[6]

---

5. See Goldberg, 282: "However wittily aware he was of his own graphic investment (an element that could lead to a 'psychoanalytic graphology') and however
brilliantly he analyzes such investment in others, Barthes nonetheless does not quite
recognize what accompanies his response to the lure of the pen—and of the hand
writing[:] logocentric complicity."
6. See Goldberg, 318, on "typewriterly" as opposed to "computerly" style: "It has
been a long time now since I wrote by hand. For many years I wrote at the typewriter.
The fantasy was that language was there in the keys and that striking them would
release the text (Michelangelo's fantasy about the stone that contained the statue,
transferred to the machine, but still a logocentric fantasy). But now the fantasy is
that somewhere there is (or someday there will be) a program, and rather than having to write oneself, the machine will be able to do it. Considering the opprobrium
that so-called 'computer prose' has already elicited, it is clear that, for some, that
day has arrived. Perhaps it is here. A machine wrote this." See also Auster and
Messer, 55–56: "The typewriter is on the kitchen table, and my hands are on the
typewriter. Letter by letter, I have watched it write these words."

Nor is he nomadic. For Barthes, writing is done at home. "I simply cannot work in a hotel room. It's not the hotel itself that bothers me. It's not a question of ambiance or decor, but of spatial organization (it's not for nothing that I'm called a structuralist!)" (180). Or rather, it's done at identical desks in identical homes:[7]

> To be able to function, I need to be able structurally to reproduce my usual work space. In Paris, the place where I work (every day from 9:30 A.M. to 1 P.M.; this regular workaday schedule for writing suits me better than an aleatory schedule, which supposes a state of continual excitement) is in my bedroom. This space is completed by a music area (I play the piano every day, at about the same time: 2:30 in the afternoon) and by a "painting" area—I say "painting" with lots of quotation marks (about once a week I perform as a Sunday painter, so I need a place to splatter paint around).
>
> In my country house, I have faithfully reproduced those three areas. It's not important that they're not in the same room. It isn't the walls but the structure that counts.
>
> But that's not all. The working space itself must also be divided into a certain number of functional microplaces. First there should be a table. (I like it to be of wood. I might say that I'm on good terms with wood.) There has to be a place on the side, another table where I can spread out the different things I'm working on. And there has to be a place for the typewriter, and a desk for my different memos, notes, "microplannings" for the next few days, "macroplannings" for the trimester, etc. (I never look at them, mind you. Their simple presence is enough.) Finally, I have my index-card system, and the slips have an equally strict format: one quarter the size of my usual sheet of paper. At least that's how they were until the day standards were readjusted within the framework of European unification (in my opinion, one of the cruelest blows of the Common Market). Luckily, I'm not *completely* obsessive. Otherwise, I would have had to redo all my cards from the time I first started writing, twenty-five years ago. (180, emphasis original)

---

7. Proust, too, replicated his work space whenever he moved. So does Karl Lagerfeld. See Albaret, 322, 324; and Lipsky-Karasz.

So is a bit of reading done there: work-related, writerly reading.

> I know that everything I read will somehow find its inevitable
> way into my work. The only problem is to keep what I read
> for amusement from interfering with reading directed toward
> my writing. The solution is very simple: the books I read for
> pleasure, for example a classic, or one of Jakobson's books on
> linguistics, which I particularly enjoy, those I read in bed at
> night before going to sleep. I read the others (as well as avant-
> garde texts) at my worktable in the morning. There is nothing
> arbitrary about this. The bed is the locus of irresponsibility.
> The table, that of responsibility. (181)

Note a central aspect of the structuralist mind-set: the thinking in
loaded oppositions like bed versus table and irresponsibility versus
responsibility.[8]

Barthes refined this description in his 1975 autobiography, where
we first learn both that his "body" is free of its "image-repertoire"
only when it establishes its work space and that this space "is the
same everywhere, patiently adapted to the pleasure of painting, writing, sorting" (*Roland Barthes,* 38).[9] Note the poststructuralist sliding
of pleasure into the—conventionally speaking—unpleasurable work
space. (Perhaps he never wrote elsewhere, unlike Bishop or Chatwin.)
We then encounter a Proustian metaphor—or Barthesian shallop:

> A frequent image: that of the ship *Argo* (luminous and
> white), each piece of which the Argonauts gradually replaced,
> so that they ended with an entirely new ship, without having
> to alter either its name or its form. This ship *Argo* is highly
> useful: it affords the allegory of an eminently structural object,
> created not by genius, inspiration, determination, evolution,
> but by two modest actions (which cannot be caught up in any

---

8. Like Bishop, Barthes never mentions drawers, which is strange for someone with
so much to hide, including his logocentrism, but not so strange for someone who
doesn't want us to know that. See Barthes, *Roland Barthes,* 156 (emphasis original):
"In what he writes, each protects his own sexuality." See also Bachelard, 78: "Wardrobes
with their shelves, desks with their drawers, and chests with their false bottoms are
veritable organs of the secret psychological life. Indeed, without these 'objects' and a
few others in equally high favor, our intimate life would lack a model of intimacy."
9. For pre-Lacanian Barthes, one's "image-repertoire" pertains to visible, pre-
symbolic order but isn't exactly "imaginary."

mystique of creation): *substitution* (one part replaces another, as in a paradigm) and *nomination* (the name is in no way linked to the stability of the parts): by dint of combinations made within one and the same name, nothing is left of the *origin: Argo* is an object with no other cause than its name, with no other identity than its form.

Another *Argo:* I have two work spaces, one in Paris, the other in the country. Between them there is no common object, for nothing is ever carried back and forth. Yet these sites are identical. Why? Because the arrangement of tools (paper, pens, desks, clocks, calendars) is the same: it is the structure of the space which constitutes its identity. (*Roland Barthes,* 46, emphasis original)

We then encounter an imaginary work space—a space Richard Howard does in fact have (as indicated in "Bedtime Story"), and a third-person description that slides into first:[10]

Working on some text which is well under way, he likes to look up details, corroborations, in works of scholarship; if he could, he would have an exemplary library of reference works (dictionaries, encyclopedias, manuals, etc.): so that scholarship would be in a circle around me, at my disposal; so that I need merely *consult* it—and not ingest it; so that scholarship be kept in its place as a *complement of writing.* (*Roland Barthes,* 158–59, emphasis original)

Note another aspect of the structuralist—not to mention humanist—mind-set: the centering of the subject, as opposed to Stephen King's decentering. Note too the refusal, in reality, to situate the text amid a referential intertext. But for some reason, possibly a prior claim upon his image-repertoire, Barthes doesn't feel like an Argonaut at his actual desk. (The only sailor with whom Barthes consciously identifies is the Flying Dutchman. To reiterate that pseudo-Lacanian passage in *A Lover's Discourse:* "I cannot stop

---

10. *Roland Barthes's* Cartesian epigraph—handwritten—reads, "It must all be considered as if spoken by a character in a novel." See also Barthes, *Writing Degree Zero,* 40: "The whole of Literature can declare *Lavartus prodeo* [Descartes's motto], As I walk forward, I point out my mask."

wandering (loving) because of an ancient sign which dedicated me, in the remote days of my earliest childhood, to the god of my Image-repertoire, afflicting me with a compulsion to speak which leads me to say 'I love you' in one port of call after another, until some other receives this phrase and gives it back to me; but no one can assume the impossible reply (of an insupportable fulfillment), and my wandering, my errantry continues" [102].) He feels like a pen there. Or rather, like a squid—a Proustian squid, although Barthes specifies a smaller species, endlessly extruding sign after sign:

> I am writing this day after day; it takes, it sets: the cuttlefish produces its ink: I tie up my image-system (in order to protect myself and at the same time to offer myself).
>
> How will I know that the book is finished? [When at] a certain moment, no further transformation is possible but the one which occurred to the ship *Argo*. I could keep the book a very long time, by gradually changing each of its fragments. (*Roland Barthes*, 163–64)

Despite having characterized both his desks and his texts as Argo-like, Barthes doesn't make—or at least doesn't make public—the obvious structural connection between them. (Another truth he'd keep to himself?) Nor does he make the metonymic connection. By "metonymic," I mean that texts are created—or constantly re-created—on desks, and that desks are constantly re-created under and around texts. (By "re-creation," I mean both revision and rearrangement, both alteration and replication.) Nor does Barthes connect the two to the body, not even to the unerotic body, which is literally there doing the re-creating (another at least metonymic connection); the body which is figuratively there freeing itself of its image-repertoire (he must have meant the intellect is doing the freeing); the body which, insofar as it constantly re-creates (replicates) itself at the cellular level, is equally Argo-like, something he never says anywhere; the body, as he does indicate later in the autobiography, which can be seen as the very "principle" of structuration (*Roland Barthes,* 175). Our bodies, our desks, our texts.

Barthes does make other connections, of course. The structural protocols relate to his somewhat obsessive character, to his sense of responsibility, to a preference for smoothness, to certain kinds of hedonism (taking pleasure in pens, investing desire in graphic impulses), and to the writer's faith in ritual or routine. (For Toni Morrison, as for many writers, the routine involves caffeine: "I always get up and make a cup of coffee while it is still dark—it must be dark—and then I drink the coffee and watch the light come. This ritual comprises my preparation to enter a space that I can only call nonsecular" [quoted in Krementz, 27].)[11] More important, they also relate both to a transvaluation of literary modesty, as opposed to genius or inspiration, and to a rather telling admission concerning at least a few of the structural components (his "micro-" and "macroplannings," or calendars): that he needn't—perhaps shouldn't—look at them.[12] Barthes implies, moreover, that the protocols concern a need for comfort, or more specifically to twin anxieties that generate the need: spatial disorientation and linguistic confusion. "To feel comfortable in a space, I must in fact be able to proceed from one reference point to another," he writes at the very end of his literary career, "and, like Robinson [Crusoe] happy on his island, to make my way in comfort from one domicile to another" ("At Le Palace Tonight . . . ," 46). "[Language] is not so much a stock of materials as a horizon, which implies both a boundary and a perspective," he writes at the beginning; "in short it is the comforting area of an ordered space" (*Writing Degree Zero,* 9).

So why doesn't Barthes connect his desks and texts? And why doesn't he connect the two to his body, by which I mean, why doesn't he connect both of them to it? (He does recognize, of course, that the writer's text—ideally speaking—inscribes his or her corporeal self: literary style should represent the sexy "grain" of the stylist's voice.)[13] The short answer to the first question is that whereas Barthes figuratively "sees" texts—as linguistic, structural,

---

11. See Dillard, 49: "I drank coffee in titrated doses. It was a tricky business, requiring the finely tuned judgment of a skilled anesthesiologist. There was a tiny range within which coffee was effective, short of which it was useless, and beyond which, fatal."

12. See *Camera Lucida,* 90, where the grief-stricken author can't have the "winter garden" photograph of his mother on his desk unless he avoids looking at it there.

13. See, e.g., Barthes, *Pleasure of the Text,* 17: "Does the text have human form, is it a figure, an anagram of the body? Yes, but of our erotic body."

and stylized—he literally fails to see his work space, by which I mean everything including the calendars placed just so. He works at desks much as ordinary people speak native languages, unaware of them as external systems.[14] The short answer to the second question is that Barthes doesn't have the same body at his otherwise-identical desks. But of course, it's the long answers I'm interested in.

Barthes first described textual opacity in *Writing Degree Zero*. Whereas classical writing was transparent, Barthes writes, "towards the end of the eighteenth century this transparency becomes clouded; literary form [now] fascinates the reader, it strikes him as exotic, it enthralls him, it acquires a weight" (3). And with Flaubert mythically "grinding away at his sentences," literature becomes "the problematics of language" (63). This cloudy problematization will include Barthes himself—that cuttlefish producing its ink—even though he'd rather it didn't: "A third vision then appears: that of infinitely spread-out languages, of parentheses never to be closed: a utopian vision in that it supposes a mobile, plural reader, who nimbly inserts and removes the quotation marks: who begins to write *with me*" (*Roland Barthes,* 161, emphasis original). What's "utopian" is that liberation from an all-too-visible image-repertoire (in other words, from the all-too-distracting ideological, stereotypical, and stylistically derivative aspects of language), a liberation his relieved "body" senses when it works at and fails to notice certain now-invisible desk arrangements. Barthes's desk, then, embodies his image-repertoire (which also happens to be what Flaubert's did for him)—"image-repertoire," that is, in Bachelard's sense, not Lacan's:

> What Lacan means by *imaginaire* is closely related to analogy, analogy between images, since the image-repertoire is . . . where the subject adheres to an image in a movement of identification that relies in particular on the coalescence of the signifier and

---

14. Barthes himself is extraordinary. "I see language," he rather uncomfortably declares. "According to an initial vision, the image-repertoire is simple: it is the discourse of others *insofar as I see it* (I put it between quotation marks). Then I turn the scopia on myself: I see my language *insofar as it is seen:* I see it *naked* (without quotation marks): this is the disgraced, pained phase of the image-repertoire" (*Roland Barthes,* 161, emphasis original). Recall the "language forest" outside of which Benjamin's translator finds herself (Benjamin, "Task," 76).

the signified. . . . I'm interested, if not in the signifier, at least in
what is called *signifiance,* which is a regime of meaning . . . that
never closes upon a signified, and where the subject . . . always
goes from signifier to signifier, through meaning, without ever
ending in closure. (Barthes, "Twenty Key Words for Roland
Barthes," 209)[15]

And the infinitely spread-out style produced there is less soft,
less smooth, and—ironically enough—even more unoriginal than
Barthes himself could have recognized.[16] By "unoriginal," I mean
Proustian.[17] As Howard has observed, "Barthes, a writer of great
persuasion and power, characteristically 'runs' to a very long sentence, a rumination held together by colons and various signs of

---

15. Barthes derives his conception of *signifiance* from Kristeva. See Kristeva, *Revolution in Poetic Language,* 17: "What we call *signifiance* [is] this unlimited and
unbounded generating process, this unceasing operation of the drives toward, in,
and through language."

16. Cf. Derrida, 40–41: "The rigor is never rigid. In fact, the supple is a category
that I take to be indispensable to any description of Barthes's manners. This virtue
of suppleness is practiced without the least trace of either labor or labor's efface-
ment. He never did without it, whether in theorization, writing strategies, or social
intercourse, and it can even be read in the graphics of his writing, which I read as
the extreme refinement of the civility he locates, in *Camera Lucida* and while speaking of his mother, at the limits of the moral and even above it. It is a suppleness that
is at once *liée,* linked, and *déliée,* unlinked, flowing, shrewd, as one says of writing
or of the mind."

17. Proust himself has a different take on literary originality, but one that nonetheless anticipates Barthes's conception of the text as "that which goes to the limit of
the rules of . . . readability" (Barthes, "From Work to Text," 157). See Proust, *In
Search of Lost Time,* 3:446: "The writer who had taken Bergotte's place in my affec-
tions wearied me not by the incoherence but by the novelty—perfectly coherent—of
associations which I was unaccustomed to following. The point, always the same,
at which I felt myself falter indicated the identity of each renewed feat of acrobat-
ics that I must undertake. Moreover, when once in a thousand times I did succeed
in following the writer to the end of his sentence, what I saw there always had a
humor, a truthfulness, and a charm similar to those which I had found long ago
in reading Bergotte, only more delightful. I reflected that it was not so many years
since a renewal of the world similar to that which I now expected his successor to
produce had been wrought for me by Bergotte himself. And I was led to wonder
whether there was any truth in the distinction which we are always making between
art, which is no more advanced now than in Homer's day, and science with its continuous progress. Perhaps, on the contrary, art was in this respect like science; each
new original writer seemed to me to have advanced beyond the stage of his immediate predecessor; and who was to say whether in twenty years' time, when I should
be able to accompany without strain or effort the newcomer of today, another might
not emerge in the face of whom the present one would go the way of Bergotte?"

equivalence ('in other words,' 'i.e.,' 'in short'); clearly he is reluctant to let his sentence go until, like Jacob's angel, it turns and blesses him" ("Translator's Note," ix–x).

Barthes rather sensibly claimed that no two men have the same body. (Unlike both Stoppard and Chatwin, he never considers twins. Not even Esau.)[18] He sees this in artwork: "What is ultimately inimitable is the body; no discourse, whether verbal or plastic . . . can reduce one body to another body. [Cy Twombly] reveals this fatality: my body will never be yours" ("Cy Twombly: Works on Paper," 170). He also sees it in collaborative work. To quote a third-person self-examination that slides into first:

> His friends on *Tel quel* . . . insist that they must agree to speak a common, general, incorporeal language, i.e., political language, *although each of them speaks it with his own body.*— Then why don't you do the same thing?—Precisely, no doubt, because I do not have the same body that they do; my body cannot accommodate itself to *generality,* to the power of generality which is language.—Isn't that an individualistic view? Wouldn't one expect to hear it from a Christian—a notorious anti-Hegelian—such as Kierkegaard?
>
> The body is the irreducible difference, and at the same time it is the principle of all structuration (since structuration is what is Unique in structure). (*Roland Barthes,* 175, emphasis original)

Not so sensibly, and working alone (or nearly alone: he lived with Mom), Barthes also claimed to have one body in town, another in the country. His urban body is "alert yet tired," his rural body "heavy yet rested," and so—it seems—they're not the same structure (*Roland Barthes,* 61). This physical (yet imaginary) experience of having different bodies at different (yet identical) desks, along with the experience of both *Tel quel* and Twombly, moreover, belie the writer's hopeful tendency elsewhere to represent his body—or rather "the" body—in singular, metaphysical, and transcendental terms. "In an author's lexicon," he asks in the autobiography, "will there not always be a word-as-mana, a word whose ardent,

---

18. Stoppard's interest in twins can be seen in *Hapgood* (in *Plays,* vol. 5), and Chatwin's in *On the Black Hill.* I discuss both texts in "Movable Type."

complex, ineffable, and somehow sacred signification gives the illusion that by this word one might answer for everything?"

> This word has gradually appeared in his work: at first it was
> masked by the instance of Truth (that of history), then by that
> of Validity (that of systems and structures); now it blossoms,
> it flourishes; this word-as-mana is the word "body." (*Roland
> Barthes,* 129–30)

"Argo," incidentally, is another such word for Barthes.[19] The experiences of corporeal differentiation also belie his hopeless tendency elsewhere to see no such distinction—or to imagine there is none. Two men do have the same body if Barthes finds them equally attractive (if they're "type"-able) or if they find one another so. "My body will never be yours," he writes of Twombly, and "from this fatality, in which a certain human affliction can be epitomized, there is only one means of escape: seduction: that my body (or its sensuous substitutes, art, writing) seduce, overwhelm, or disturb the other body" ("Cy Twombly," 170). One such elsewhere is sexy, heterosexually perceived Italy, where certain women, at least for Stendhal, are interchangeable.[20] Another is sexy, homosexually perceived France, where for Barthes certain men are.[21] Yet an-

---

19. See *Roland Barthes,* 127: "A word, a figure of thought, a metaphor, in short, a form fastens upon him for several years, he repeats it, uses it everywhere (for instance, 'body,' 'difference,' 'Orpheus,' 'Argo,' etc.), but he makes no effort to reflect further as to what he means by such words or such figures."

20. See Barthes, "One Always Fails in Speaking of What One Loves," 298 (emphasis original), probably the last text he wrote: "What is loved and indeed what is enjoyed [by Stendhal] are collections, concomitances: contrary to the romantic project of *Amour fou,* it is not Woman who is adorable in Italy, but always Women; it is not *a* pleasure which Italy affords, it is a simultaneity, an overdetermination of pleasures: La Scala, the veritable eidetic locus of Italian delights, is not a theater in the word's banally functional sense (to see what is represented); it is a polyphony of pleasures: the opera itself, the ballet, the conversation, the gossip, love, and ices (*gelati, crepe,* and *pezzi duri*). This amorous plural, analogous to that enjoyed today by someone 'cruising,' is evidently a Stendhalian principle: it involves an implicit theory of *irregular discontinuity* which can be said to be simultaneously aesthetic, psychological, and metaphysical; plural passion, as a matter of fact—once its excellence has been acknowledged—necessitates leaping from one object to another, as chance presents them, without experiencing the slightest sentiment of guilt with regard to the disorder such a procedure involves."

21. See Barthes, "Soirées de Paris," 73 (emphasis original): "I played the piano a little for O., after he asked me to, knowing at that very moment that I had to give

other is Japan, where he's more comfortable cruising but not at all comfortable in the language.[22]

There are two reasons why Barthes situates his erotic body and not his intellect as image-repertoire-free when writing, even though that body—ideally speaking—isn't unique. The first reason concerns his having been an unhappy homosexual: Barthes never really felt successful at seduction, nor at being seduced, and so never experienced sexual uniformity. He could only imagine it. The second reason concerns both the Cartesian mind/body opposition and a transvaluation thereof. The erotic body—even, potentially, Barthes's own erotic body—may be neither unique nor original, but the writer's mind is even less so. That mind is yet another Argo, overwhelmed by tidal waves of other writers' language. So it is the body, by default, and not the mind where liberation—hence either literary or critical distinction—can be located. Barthes, of course, claims not to value such distinction, or at least wants to convince himself he doesn't. (Sour grapes.) Having anticipated the intertextual revolution as early as 1953 with *Writing Degree Zero,* Barthes helped launch it in 1968 with "The Death of the Author," where he declares that "writing is the destruction of every voice, of every point of origin." Writing, he writes, "is that neutral, composite, oblique space where our subject slips away, the negative where all identity is lost, starting with the very identity of the body writing" (142).[23] Having buried the

him up; how lovely his eyes were then, and his gentle face, made gentler by his long hair: a delicate but inaccessible and enigmatic creature, sweet-natured yet remote. Then I sent him away, saying I had work to do, knowing it was over, and that more than Olivier was over: the love of *one* boy."

22. See Barthes, *Empire of Signs,* 97–98 (emphasis original): "All Japanese (and not: Asiatics) form a general body (but not a total one, as we assume from our Occidental distance), and yet a vast tribe of different bodies, each of which refers to a class, which vanishes, without disorder, in the direction of an interminable order; in a word: open, to the last moment, like a logical system. The result—or the stake—of this dialectic is the following: the Japanese body achieves the limit of its individuality (like the Zen master when he *invents* a preposterous and upsetting answer to the disciple's serious and banal question), but this individuality cannot be understood in the Western sense; it is pure of all hysteria, does not aim at making the individual into an original body, distinguished from other bodies, inflamed by that promotional fever which infects the West."

23. The word "intertextuality" originates with Kristeva, not Barthes. See Kristeva, "Word, Dialogue, and Novel."

author, moreover, "the modern scriptor can thus no longer be-lieve . . . that this hand is too slow for his thought or passion and that consequently, making a law of necessity, he must emphasize this delay and indefinitely 'polish' his form" (146):

> For him, on the contrary, the hand, cut off from any voice,
> borne by a pure gesture of inscription (and not of expression),
> traces a field without origin—or which, at least, has no other
> origin than language itself, language which ceaselessly calls into
> question all origins.
>
> We know now that a text is not a line of words releasing a
> single "theological" meaning (the "message" of the Author-God)
> but a multidimensional space in which a variety of writings,
> none of them original, blend and clash. The text is a tissue of
> quotations drawn from the innumerable centers of culture.
> Similar to Bouvard and Pécuchet, those eternal copyists, at once
> sublime and comic and whose profound ridiculousness indi-
> cates precisely the truth of writing, the writer can only imitate
> a gesture that is always anterior, never original. ("Death of the
> Author," 146)

Nor did Barthes ever renounce the revolution, despite the fact that, like any writer, he always had an overwhelming if futile need to inscribe himself alone, whoever or whatever—real or imaginary; unary, binary, or multitudinous—that self may be.[24] Or at least, he never did until the end of his life.

Notice the tonal shift from resignation to celebration in the following treatments of a supposedly intersubjective intertextuali-ty. The presentation is chronological. Notice too how Barthes's egocentrism rears its head, looks around, and gradually discovers the alibi of embodiment—an alibi that enables the celebration insofar as it secretly signifies originality. Then notice a final shift—to frustration if not to full-fledged defiance—as the ego-centric author, now approaching his literal death, rejects both intertextuality and the alibi. Although one can "select such and such a mode of writing, and in so doing . . . aspire to the freshness

---

24. See Smith, 108: For Barthes, "any identary 'I' [is] nothing more than a fictional representation, a colligation and a suturing of a collection of imaginary identities."

of novelty," young Barthes first observed in *Writing Degree Zero*, it is impossible to develop it "without gradually becoming a prisoner of someone else's words and even of [one's] own" (17). For the writer newly aware of this, the feeling is less than playful, let alone joyous. It's pathetic, "tragic" even (86). (Think of the writing crisis that sends Thomas Mann's Aschenbach—prisoner of his own words—to a lonely death in Venice. Think too of how young Mann was at the time.) Barthes had lost that tragic feeling by 1964, when, notwithstanding the influence other writers, Proust in particular, have clearly had on his work, he playfully claimed not to know what an "influence" was.[25] To his mind, the mind of one who now clearly enjoys working with language and form, "what is transmitted is not 'ideas' but 'languages,' i.e., forms which can be filled in different fashions" ("I Don't Believe in Influences," 26–27).[26] Then, in 1972 (four years after "The Death of the Author"), Barthes blissfully explains why the pleasure of the text includes the author's "amicable return." By "pleasure," here, he means the joy of bedridden reading, not writing:

> It really would be a wonderful liberation to be able to take up the authors of the past again as agreeable, charming bodies, traces which still remain seductive. There are writers who point the way for us: Proust, Jean Genet (I'm thinking of his novels)—he is in his books. He says, *I, Jean*. It would never occur to anyone, however, to say that his books express a subjective experience: Genet is in his books as a *paper character*. ("Pleasure/Writing/Reading," 166, emphasis original)

In other words, the return of the author—presumably fictive, or imaginary—is amicable because corporeal. Barthes further sexualizes

---

25. See *Pleasure of the Text*, 36 (emphasis original): "I recognize that Proust's work, for myself at least, is *the* reference work, the general *mathesis*, the *mandala* of the entire literary cosmogony."

26. See Barthes, "Style and Its Image," 98–99 (emphasis original): "[We should] consider stylistic features as *transformations*, derived either from collective formulas (of unrecoverable origin, literary or pre-literary) or, by metaphoric interplay, from idiolectal forms; in both cases, what should govern the stylistic task is the search for models, for patterns; sentential structures, syntagmatic clichés, divisions and clausulae of sentences; and what should animate this task is the conviction that style is essentially a citational procedure, a body of formulas, a memory (almost in the cybernetic sense of the word), an inheritance based on culture and not on expressivity."

this corporeality in 1973. Now addressing the joy of desk-bound writing, he situates truth "in the hand which presses down and traces a line, i.e., in *the body which throbs* (which takes pleasure)" ("Masson's Semiography," 154, emphasis original). Barthes specifies this sexualization in *The Pleasure of the Text:* "I write because I do not want the words I find," he writes (40). (But who'd reject those signifiers, let alone signifieds? This is how all writers feel, and how we'd say it.)

> And at the same time, this *next-to-last language* is the language of my pleasure: for hours on end I read Zola, Proust, Verne, *The Count of Monte Cristo,* the *Memoirs of a Tourist,* and sometimes even Julian Green. This is my pleasure, but not my bliss: bliss may come only with the *absolutely* new, for only the new disturbs (weakens) consciousness (easy? not at all: nine times out of ten, the new is only the stereotype of novelty). (*Pleasure of the Text,* 40, emphasis original)

In other words, the throbbing body is the orgasmic, masturbatory body so readily linked to selfless yet self-assertive writing, and not, Barthes now insists, to reading. Or at least not linked to leisurely reading done in bed and away from the desk. Of work-related, writerly reading done at it—reading also written about there—Barthes explains, "Whenever I attempt to 'analyze' a text which has given me pleasure, it is not my 'subjectivity' I encounter but my 'individuality,' the given which makes my body separate from other bodies and appropriates its suffering or its pleasure: it is my body of bliss I encounter" (62).[27]

Theoretical bliss, that is. In practice, this kind of writing is both exhausting and difficult. "'I' is harder to write than to read,"

---

27. See Smith, xxxv (emphasis original) for a relevant distinction between "subjectivity" and "individuality": "The human *agent* will be seen here [in *Discerning the Subject*] as the place from which resistance to the ideological is produced or played out, and thus as *not* equivalent to either the 'subject' or the 'individual.' 'The individual' will be understood here as simply the illusion of whole and coherent personal organization, or as the misleading description of the imaginary ground on which different subject-positions are colligated. And thence the commonly used term 'subject' will be broken down and will be understood as the term inaccurately used to describe what is actually the series or the conglomeration of *positions,* subject-positions, provisional and not necessarily indefeasible, into which a person is called momentarily by the discourses and the world that he/she inhabits. The term 'agent,'

Barthes wearily admits in an admittedly egocentric journal entry probably made in Paris, definitely in 1977 ("Deliberation," 366).[28] And so it has become a matter of "indifference" to him whether or not he's modern; he's "like a blind man whose finger gropes along the text of life, here and there recognizing 'what has already been said'" (367). It has even become a matter of indifference whether or not he writes any way at all: "I am both too big and too weak for writing," writes Barthes in *A Lover's Discourse* (a collaborative text done by both conversing with and cruising students). "I am *alongside it,* for writing is always dense, violent, indifferent to the infantile ego which solicits it."

> I cannot *write myself.* What, after all, is this "I" who would write himself? Even as he would enter into the writing, the writing would take the wind out of his sails, would render him null and void—futile; a gradual dilapidation would occur, in which the other's image, too, would be gradually involved (to write *on* something is to outmode it), a disgust whose conclusion could only be: *what's the use?* What obstructs amorous writing is the illusion of expressivity: as a writer, or assuming myself to be one, I continue to fool myself as to the *effects* of language: I do not know that the word "suffering" expresses no suffering and that, consequently, to use it is not only to communicate nothing but even, and immediately, to annoy, to irritate (not to mention the absurdity). (98, emphasis original)

One year later, however, he finds Proust's conception of the "I" who writes himself both influential and energizing. (Maybe he was out of town at the time.) Proust's "I"—now Barthes's as well—represents his best, possibly unconscious, and hence truest

---

by contrast, will be used to mark the idea of a form of subjectivity where, by virtue of the contradictions and disturbances in and among subject-positions, the possibility (indeed, the actuality) of resistance to ideological pressure is allowed for (even though that resistance too must be produced in an ideological context)."

28. Shouldn't the journal, Barthes asks himself, "be considered and practiced as that form which essentially expresses the inessentials of the world, the world as inessential?" For that, "the Journal's subject would have to be the world, and not me; otherwise, what is uttered is a kind of egotism which constitutes a screen between the world and the writing; whatever I do, I become consistent, confronting the world which is not so. How to keep a Journal without egotism? That is precisely the question which keeps me from writing one (for I have had just about enough egotism)" ("Deliberation," 370).

self. "The Proustian *oeuvre* brings on stage (or into writing) an 'I'
[who] is not the one who remembers, confides, confesses; he is the
one who discourses," discourses Barthes. "[So] it is vain to wonder
if the book's Narrator is Proust (in the civil meaning of the pat-
ronymic): it is simply *another* Proust, often unknown to himself"
(*"Longtemps, je me suis couché de bonne heure . . . ,"* 282, emphasis
original). This, of course, is a discovery many writers make even if
they haven't read *À la recherche du temps perdu.* Barthes's Proustian
"I" also represents his unique self, not his unique body. Observe
the renunciation:

> Hence I shall be speaking of "myself." "Myself" is to be under-
> stood here in the full sense: not the asepticized substitute of a
> general reader (any substitution is an asepsis); I shall be speaking
> of the one for whom no one else can be substituted, for better
> or worse. It is the *intimate* which seeks utterance in me, seeks to
> make its cry heard, confronting generality, confronting science.
> (*"Longtemps,"* 284, emphasis original)

That "I" also fashions uniquely modern writing—if only in relation to the author's earlier extrusions: "One of these days I should
like to develop . . . this loving or amorous power . . . either by
means of an Essay . . . or by means of a Novel, it being understood that for convenience's sake this is what I am calling any
Form which is new in relation to my past practice, to my past
discourse" (288).[29] Our bodies, our desks, our texts—and yes, at
last, our selves.

That reference to *Bouvard and Pécuchet* in "The Death of the
Author" doesn't indicate the full significance of Flaubert's unfinished novel. Those eternal copyists, whose profound ridiculous-
ness indicates the truth of writing insofar as they merely parrot
languages that originate elsewhere, have telling work habits as well.
On the one hand, Barthes finds their protocols of writing both cir-
cumscribed and déclassé—as does Flaubert. Unlike the Japanese
stationery store, Barthes writes, the French corollary "remains a

---

29. Cf. Mann, 10: "With time, an element of official pedagogy entered into Gustav
Aschenbach's productions; in later years his style dispensed with forthright audaci-
ties, with subtle new nuances; he transformed himself into the exemplary established author, the polished traditionalist, conservative, formal, even formulaic."

papeterie of . . . scribes." Its exemplary product is the "calligraphed duplicate." (So much for that graphic impulse.) Its exemplary patrons are Bouvard and Pécuchet (*Empire of Signs*, 85). (True writers, it seems, shop elsewhere. Of course, where that is depends upon where you are: The British Chatwin, writing in *moleskine* notebooks made in France, found *papeterie* sufficiently exotic for his obsessive needs.) On the other hand, Barthes finds Bouvard and Pécuchet uncanny. Back at home, that is, where they sit face to face at a partners desk, these two replicate Barthes's own double work space. Or Barthes replicates theirs, a structural equivalence our "paper character" may fail to notice precisely because he'd rather not imagine himself a mere copyist.

Who copies, or replicates, whom? Is there ever an original? By now, we're used to celebrating the extent to which the first question has no definite answer and the answer to the second is a definite "no." Postmodernity, according to Baudrillard impersonators, is composed of simulacra. Gender and sexuality, queer theorists endlessly repeat themselves, are performative copies of imaginary originals. (Even Judith Butler, the poststructuralist presumed to have said so first, is no original: We forget Mary McIntosh. And then there's Adorno: "The human is indissolubly linked with imitation: a human being only becomes human at all by imitating other human beings" [154].) For Barthes, however, the answers weren't that obvious. When I announced that his desks and texts are homologous substitutions for the writer's body, itself a substitution for his subjectivity, I was indicating a distinction that Barthes himself thought he'd discovered and that transcends his related, image-repertoire-oriented division between Bachelard and Lacan: the distinction between—and transvaluation of—analogy and homology. (Barthes, you recall, deplored the analogous sliding of signifiers into signifieds that he found in Lacan and appreciated the homologous sliding from signifier to signifier—*signifiance*—that he found in Bachelard.) "What stands in beneficent opposition to perfidious Analogy," he writes in the autobiography, "is simple structural correspondence: *Homology,* which reduces the recall of the first object to a proportional allusion" (*Roland Barthes,* 44, emphasis original). Like Foucault giddily transvaluing "resemblance" and "similitude" in *This Is Not a Pipe* (a monograph on

Magritte) or like Bishop less giddily transforming Baudelaire's sense of "correspondence" in "The Bight" (via her punning correspondence of figurative correspondence to literal correspondence, or letter writing), Barthes is being transgressive on purpose. His "body," or subjectivity, may still have its "sensuous substitutes" or derivatives (artwork, work space), but such copies themselves are both interchangeable and intertextual. The transgression, of course, is against logocentrism, which privileges original over copy, signified over signifier, speech over writing, presence over absence, and so on, and which depends upon a number of related predications (transparent as opposed to opaque, centered versus decentered, immobile versus mobile, full versus empty).[30] Barthes himself recognized this as well as the basic futility of the move, which may be why—ironically enough—he sought literary antecedents in like-minded writers. Michelet, with his various "paired themes," may have been the first such writer—as well as the last (Barthes, *Michelet*, 211). Here is Barthes in 1954, extolling Michelet's related transvaluation of union and unity:

> Union is an inferior state because it merely compounds positive elements which it can harmonize but not abolish. Unity is superior to it, insofar as it destroys the very memory of the constitutive individualities and elicits in their place a zone of absence, in which everything is once again possible. (*Michelet*, 28)[31]

Here he is in 1974, extolling Michelet's passion for equivalence: "What gives Michelet his high standing . . . is that in his entire

---

30. See Barthes, *Empire of Signs*, 78–79: "In the West, the mirror is an essentially narcissistic object: man conceives a mirror only in order to look at himself in it; but in the Orient, apparently, the mirror is empty; it is the symbol of the very emptiness of symbols."

31. Cf. Barthes, "Death of the Author," 148 (emphasis original), on the "unity" of the text: "Thus is revealed the total existence of writing: a text is made of multiple writings, drawn from many cultures and entering into mutual relations of dialogue, parody, contestation, but there is one place where this multiplicity is focused and that place is the reader, not, as was hitherto said, the author. The reader is that space on which all the quotations that make up a writing are inscribed without any of them being lost; a text's unity lies not in its origin but in its destination. Yet this destination cannot any longer be personal: the reader is without history, biography, psychology; he is simply that *someone* who holds together in a single field all the traces by which the written text is constituted."

oeuvre . . . symbolic equivalence is a systematic path of knowledge. . . . When, for example, Michelet tells us, literally, that
'*coffee is the alibi of sex*' he formulates a new logic which flourishes
today in all knowledge" ("Michelet's Modernity," 209, emphasis
original).[32]

But the privileging of homology is halfhearted at best. Given
Barthes's egocentrism—his ineradicable desire to be original, his
ungovernable devotion to humanist subjectivity—analogy and substitution remain valuable to him. Stylish writing incorporates "the
grain of the voice" just when it shouldn't—just when, for example,
it might be said instead to encrypt the unconscious. Journal writing
remains problematically "inauthentic" just when it shouldn't, by
which Barthes—probably thinking of himself "suffering"—doesn't
mean "that someone who expresses himself in one is not sincere";
rather,

> I mean that its very form can only be borrowed from an ante-
> cedent and motionless Form (that, precisely, of the Intimate
> Journal), which cannot be subverted. Writing my Journal, I
> am, by status, doomed to simulation. A double simulation, in
> fact: for since every emotion is a copy of the same emotion one
> has read somewhere, to report a mood in the coded language
> of the Collection of Moods is to copy a copy: even if the text
> was "original," it would already be a copy; all the more so if it
> is familiar, worn, threadbare. ("Deliberation," 371)

And the most valuable analogy of all—due in part, quite possibly,
to the obvious metonymic connection between working at a desk
and doing something other than either reading, sleeping, seduc-
ing, eating marzipan (to cite Benjamin), or (to cite Michelet, not
Morrison) drinking coffee in bed nearby—is the (phallogocentric)
analogy (or "alliance," to cite Jonathan Goldberg on Derrida on
Rousseau [291]) between writing and masturbating.

---

32. The term "alibi" has a positive valence in this passage. This is unusual for
Barthes, who ordinarily sees alibis as ideological. See *Mythologies*. See also *Pleasure
of the Text*, 55–56 (emphasis original): "Figuration is the way in which the erotic
body appears (to whatever degree and in whatever form that may be) in the profile
of the text. . . . Representation, on the other hand, is *embarrassed figuration,* encum-
bered with other meanings than that of desire: a space of alibis (reality, morality,
likelihood, readability, truth, etc.)."

Like masturbating, writing for Barthes—notwithstanding his willingness to write about the process, notwithstanding his intention to publish—is a solitary, private, almost furtive pleasure. (Both activities, moreover, involve being on good terms with "wood.") That's the basic reason why, like Proust, he works in his bedroom.[33] (The first use of *"recherche"* in *À la recherche* does concern masturbation.) It's the basic reason why the work involves keeping purportedly unconventional truths to himself, truths such as: The embodiment alibi secretly signifies originality. It's the secret reason why favorite writers, Proust in particular, are seen as nonconversational. It's why he associates writing with musical amateurism: playing for oneself alone and fantasizing perfection (and maybe even an audience), as opposed to performing perfectly well in public—something only virtuosos do.[34] Masturbatory writing, like masturbation itself, is also a relatively sad, lonely pleasure for Barthes—although not as sad and lonely as either cruising or cruisy writing are. ("Chatty" Chatwin, in this sense, was both a successful cruiser and a successfully cruisy writer, making and hallucinating connections wherever and whenever he happened to want sex or to address the reader.) "To know that one does not write for the other," Barthes tells himself and those student collaborators in *A Lover's Discourse*, "to know that these things I am going to write will never cause me to be loved by the one I love (the other), to know that writing compensates for nothing, sublimates nothing, that it is precisely *there where you are not*—this is the beginning of writing" (100, emphasis original). Derrida noticed Barthes's sadness too: "a sadness that was cheerful yet weary, desperate, lonely, [and] refined" (36).

Sad and lonely, but also relatively neat—which makes both the writing and the masturbating weary yet cheerful. When I play with myself, to be as exhibitionist as Barthes writing about writing, I never make the kind of mess that sex with other people requires. (Unless, of course, I'm also drinking coffee.) Nor do I

---

33. Stoppard, the subject of "Lightning Strikes," writes in his kitchen; Chatwin, the subject of "Movable Type," in other people's homes—both relatively public domains.
34. See *Pleasure of the Text*, 16: "On the stage of the text, no footlights: there is not, behind the text, someone active (the writer) and out front someone passive (the reader); there is not a subject and an object."

make one when I write. Barthes, I imagine, both worked and played the same way. I mean I *know* he worked that way. Among other activities there, Barthes adapted his desk to the pleasure of sorting. So I suppose he played that way as well: arranging his desk as an image-repertoire-free zone, writing a bit, going back to his irresponsible bed, not reading any Chateaubriand or Jakobson (too early for that), retrieving a favorite photograph unaccountably eroticized (or "mobilized") by some *punctum* (whereby the singularity of the other addresses me), undoing his belt, and then, well, you get the drift.[35] Picture an immobilized Argonaut. Then cleaning up, rearranging himself, rearranging the bed, hiding the photo, going back to the desk, and getting back to the equally pen-ile work of sign extrusion. Now, in town, somewhat enervated by the somewhat egocentric interlude. Now, in the country, somewhat energized.

But where are we, really, when we masturbate?[36] And who are we? Who when we write? Who, rather, are we pretending to be?

---

35. See Barthes, *Camera Lucida*, 57–59: "The presence (the dynamics) of this blind field is, I believe, what distinguishes the erotic photograph from the pornographic photograph. Pornography ordinarily represents the sexual organs, making them into a motionless object (a fetish), flattered like an idol that does not leave its niche; for me, there is no *punctum* in the pornographic image; at most it amuses me (and even then, boredom follows quickly). The erotic photograph, on the contrary (and this is its very condition), does not make the sexual organs into a central object; it may very well not show them at all; it takes the spectator outside its frame, and it is there that I animate this photograph and that it animates me."
36. See Laplanche and Pontalis, 26: In fantasy, the subject "cannot be assigned any fixed place."

LIGHTNING STRIKES

> Contrary to the narrative, which reduces the historian's body
> to the rank of an object, the *tableau* (the overview) placed
> Michelet virtually in God's position, for God's chief power
> is precisely to hold in a simultaneous perception moments,
> events, men, and causes which are humanly dispersed
> through time, space, or different orders.
>
> —*Barthes,* Michelet

U NLIKE BARTHES, Tom Stoppard has never claimed not to be intellectual.[1] In fact, he's even more intellectual, not to mention witty, than Shaw, a playwright to whom, notwithstanding political differences, he's often compared. Nor has Stoppard ever prioritized originality.[2] In fact, he'd even have us recognize his dependence

---

1. Asked about his athletic ability, Stoppard replied, "I was always an intellectual from the word go" (quoted in Gussow, 19).

2. See Nietzsche, 255–56 (emphasis original): "The poet expresses the general higher opinions possessed by a people, he is their flute and mouthpiece—but, by virtue of metric and all the other methods of art, he expresses them in such a way that the people receive them as something quite new and marvelous and believe in all serious-ness that the poet is the mouthpiece of the gods. Indeed, in the clouds of creation the poet himself forgets whence he has acquired all his spiritual wisdom—from his father and mother, from teachers and books of all kinds, from the street and especially from the priests; he is deceived by his own art and, in naive ages, really does believe that a *god* is speaking through him, that he is creating in a state of religious illumination— whereas he is repeating only what he has learned, popular wisdom mixed up with popular folly. Thus, insofar as the poet really is *vox populi* he *counts* as *vox dei*." Cf. Nietzsche, 261 (emphasis original): "Not that a man sees something new as the first one to do so, but that he sees something old, familiar, seen but overlooked by every-one, *as though it were new,* is what distinguishes true originality. The first discoverer is usually that quite commonplace and mindless fantasist—chance."

on—not to mention mastery of—an impressive number of impressive precursors, including Shaw.[3] "I have this feeling that I could have written most other people's plays and most other people could have written mine," he once claimed, "because I know how it's done and they know how it's done" (quoted in Gussow, 21).

Like Barthes, however, Stoppard has described his protocols of writing. In a 1988 interview, we first learn he has an almost Barthesian relation to writing instruments: "I write with a fountain pen; you can't scribble with a typewriter" (quoted in Guppy, 185).[4] We then learn both where he does his work and when:

> I have a very nice long room, which used to be the stable. It has a desk and lots of paper, etc. But most of my plays are written on the kitchen table at night, when everybody has gone to bed and I feel completely at peace. During the day, somehow I don't get much done; although I have a secretary who answers the phone, I always want to know who it is, and I generally get distracted. (191–92)[5]

(You'll recall that Bishop did some of her best work "standing up in the kitchen in the middle of the night" [quoted in Millier, 544] and that most writers abandon studies too organized, too disorganized, or simply too familiar to work in.) The secretary also takes dictation, transcribing plays.[6] In an interview conducted the

3. See Kelly, 11: Stoppard's spectator "collaborates in anticipating and then recognizing familiar but transformed texts as these evoke and critique major works of the western tradition." And see Gritten: Asked about a *Travesties* revival, Stoppard complained, "The play is full of allusions [that] people in their twenties [don't] recognize." See also Sammells (on Stoppard's use of Wilde) and Levenson (on his use of Shakespeare).

4. Stoppard did use a typewriter as a young journalist. "[When] I have to write in longhand," he explained at the time, "I seem to lose all sense of criticism and style" (quoted in Nadel, 115).

5. The forsaken furniture is a partners desk, one indication of the playwright's belief in both double identities and dual personalities. I discuss double identities below, dual personalities in "Movable Type."

6. See Adorno, 212: "Dictating is not only more comfortable, more conducive to concentration, it has an additional substantive benefit. Dictation makes it possible for the writer, in the earliest phases of production, to maneuver himself into the position of critic. What he sets down is tentative, provisional, mere material for revision, yet appears to him, once transcribed, as something estranged and in some measure objective. He need have no fear of committing something inadequate to paper, for he is not the one who has to write it: he outwits responsibility in its interests."

following year, we learn about another distraction—one Stoppard finds nonetheless helpful:

> Suddenly he strides over to the stereo in the corner [of the living room]; a moment later, John Lennon is singing "Mother," the song in which he indulges in a lot of primal screaming at the end. "I just wanted to tell you this," Stoppard says, rather sweetly. "I tend to write each play to one record." And then, noticing my face, "Oh! I *knew* you'd be interested."
>
> "Yes, we journalists like that sort of thing," I say. "How does it work?"
>
> "Yes, well, I just kept playing this while I was writing *Jumpers.* It has nothing to do with the play, of course, but I always find it an extraordinarily moving track. For *Hapgood,* I listened to two or three tracks of *Graceland*—you know, Paul Simon—interminably, for three or four months. And with *Rosencrantz [and Guildenstern Are Dead]* there were two Bob Dylan tracks, 'Like a Rolling Stone' and 'Subterranean Homesick Blues,' which is a lyric I've admired ever since. I *adore* it. It's one of those moments that gets to me better than even reading."
>
> "You play this stuff while you work?" I ask.
>
> "Well, in a way it stops me working. I stop and I go through the dialogue with this music on, and then I realize that it's just self-indulgence and turn it off. Work is really what one should do, isn't it?" And he clicks off the stereo and stands silently by the fireplace for a moment, as if pondering that daunting truth. (Schiff, 213–14, emphasis original)

As with Barthes, the descriptions make sense. It makes sense that a playwright would be more comfortable working in a relatively public space than in a relatively private one. (Stoppard also admits to addressing an ideal spectator, "someone more sharpwitted and attentive than the average theatergoer" [quoted in Guppy, 186]. I have a similar audience in mind.) It makes sense that he needs to read dialogue aloud. It makes sense that he finds emotional music inspirational, although I can't reconcile the image of Stoppard in that otherwise-peaceful kitchen after everyone has gone to bed with an image of him blaring Lennon there. Unless of course it's an enormous home, or he wears headphones.[7]

You may be wondering what that kitchen table looks like. Given Stoppard's classicism, I imagine it as orderly. I also imagine it as having a secret compartment. Stoppard, an autodidact who feels his self-instruction has always lagged behind his writing, once confessed that all his time "is spent concealing what I don't know" (quoted in Schiff, 214). (I do recognize the Socratic irony of this witticism. I also recognize that all such confessions should be viewed critically. For Paul de Man, they're basically exculpatory. For Foucault, they're illusory. For Barthes, the sincerity they supposedly require is "merely a second-degree image-repertoire" ["Deliberation," 360]. For Salinger's Buddy, no confession has ever been written that didn't stink a little bit of the writer's pride in having given up his pride, and so the thing to listen for with a public confessor is what he's not confessing to.) But I must confess I don't know—and, more to the point, have failed to discover— what that table looks like. Nor do I care, because what concerns me now is how Stoppard dramatizes this kind of furniture. The tables in his stage plays tend to assemble objects that indicate the knowledge certain characters strive to obtain—knowledge often pertaining to literary figures and to poets in particular. As such, they both resemble and correspond to the stage itself. The tables also correspond to dramatic irony, with characters either oblivious of the objects or simply mistaken as to their significance.[8] Think of Edgar Allan Poe's "purloined letter," then Marie Bonaparte's, and then Lacan's.

Before turning to the plays, however, it's important to know a couple of things. Stoppard believes in dramatic irony, but not for everyone. He does tend to write plays "about people who don't know very much about what's going on" and to like it "when the

---

7. Stoppard's method of working prior to *Rosencrantz and Guildenstern Are Dead* involved "ineffectual inefficiency": a "basement retreat" with a "warped table and wonky anglepoise [desk lamp], more angles than poise, a fair imitation of an impoverished writer's work space and a fair imitation of an impoverished writer" (quoted in Nadel, 114).

8. Other writers analogize desks to museums, file cabinets, and computers—all memory banks. See, e.g., Pelz.

audience is ahead of the character" (quoted in Gussow, 4, 121).[9]
But he loves it when only a portion of the audience is—as do I.
The sharper portion, that is: those of you who catch the literary
allusions and aren't necessarily positioned in the most expensive,
least elevated seats.[10] Stoppard also believes in absolute truth, but
not for anyone.[11] He doesn't share Nietzsche's conception of truth
as both subjective and relative. (Not that relativists can't imagine
tabletops his way: Foucault, for example, describes the epistemo-
logical field as "a homogeneous and neutral space in which things
could be placed so as to display at the same time the continuous
order of their identities or differences as well as the semantic field of
their denomination" [xviii].) Nor does Stoppard share Barthes's—
and Wilde's—conception of truth as both unconventional and
incommunicable.[12] Nor, notwithstanding his dialectical turn of
mind, does he locate truth in between opposing positions. Simply
put, Stoppard is more Socratic than Aristotelian, which is why
he associates the awareness of absolute truth, or omniscience, with
what he calls "a ceiling view of a situation" (quoted in Gussow, 3).
This, of course, resembles the "superior vantage point" from which
Bishop conducts aerial reconnaissance in "12 O'Clock News," but

---

9. *Rosencrantz and Guildenstern Are Dead* is the paradigmatic example of such a play.
According to Stoppard: "The chief interest and objective was to exploit a situation
which seemed to me to have enormous dramatic and comic potential—of these two
guys who in Shakespeare's context don't really know what they're doing. The little
they are told is mainly lies, and there's no reason to suppose that they ever find out
why they are killed" (quoted in Hudson, Itzin, and Trussler, 57).
10. See Gussow, 122, quoting Stoppard on the original production of *Indian Ink:*
"It was clear last night [that two characters had spent the night together], and the
reason it was clear was, she woke up in bed wearing his shawl. We did that two
nights. The first time the audience didn't notice. It's extraordinary what the audience refuse[s] to notice or to listen to. She gets up in the morning and she's wrapped
up in the shawl the painter had been wearing. It was some kind of browny orange
dull color, and last night we made it red, deep unmistakable red. Afterwards I
said to [the director], I think that's the version for dunces. He agreed. . . . I believe
there's a search on for the precise color which will leave half the audience completely
in the dark and the other half completely certain. I discuss this love affair below.
See also Brater, 205: Stoppard is drama for "the A-level and AP-English crowd,"
the audience "that knows [the] traditional canon backwards and forwards." And
see Sammells, 108: Stoppard's audience is both "literate enough to recognize [the
allusions and] flattered to be asked."
11. See Stoppard, "But for the Middle Classes."
12. See Kopelson, "Wilde, Barthes, and the Orgasmics of Truth."

without the verbal irony or misrecognition.[13] ("Quite ordered, seen from above," observes the suicide in *Albert's Bridge*—a radio play I won't discuss [Stoppard, *Plays*, 2:78].) He associates such a vantage point, moreover, with what Barthes calls "God's position" (*Michelet*, 22). Stoppard, of course, is fully cognizant of the difference—as well as the tension—between godlike omniscience and dramatic irony. Audience members may know more than characters do, but they don't know everything there is to know. (Not even Stoppard knows everything: It took him forever to learn the identities of the dead bodies in *The Real Inspector Hound* and *Jumpers*.)[14] They may overlook the stage from those relatively inexpensive seats—just as working writers overlook their desktops at more or less the same angle, although I'm not sure Stoppard is aware of the correspondence—but they don't really enjoy what Barthes calls a perpendicular "overview." (Overlook, that is, in the sense of gaze down upon, not fail to see.) Like Michelet, we merely approximate God's position.

Stoppard's work falls into two overlapping categories: short entertainments in which the nominal investigators tend to be policemen, and dialectical argument plays. I'll describe three entertainments before considering argument plays. The presentation is chronological, as in "Same Place Twice." So if the remainder of this chapter—a set of extremely close readings—seems chaotic, consider it a function of Stoppard's complexity as well as of the way I think at the keyboard. It's also a function of my desire to dramatize both chaos theory and Stoppard's theology. As with *Arcadia*'s hermit, there's method to the madness. As for his creator, God is in the details. And should such reading prove mind-boggling and

---

13. See Rabinowitz: Stoppard's only novel presents a "ceiling view" at the authorial level.

14. See, e.g., Stoppard, *Plays*, 1:xii: "Looking back at *Hound*, I can't see the point of starting to write it if one didn't know the one thing which, more than any other, made the play worth writing: that Higgs was dead and under the sofa. When the idea came it seemed an amazing piece of luck, and I constantly remember that because my instinct, even now, is to want to know more about the unwritten play than is knowable, or good to know. So, whenever I finally set off again, knowing far too little and trusting in luck, I always gain courage from remembering the wonderful day when Moon and Birdboot led the lagging author to the discovery that—of course!—'It's Higgs!'" Compare his attitude to that of Lydia Davis: "This novel is like a puzzle with a difficult solution" (*End of the Story*, 87).

tiresome—recall the "content obliquity" of Proust—rest assured there's almost none in "Movable Type."

There's no desk in *The Real Inspector Hound* (1968). There is, however, a stage. We're watching drama critics named Moon and Birdboot watching, discussing, and even participating in a convoluted murder mystery. (Their relatively expensive seats are in the front row. Stoppard's allusion, relatively easy to catch given her popularity, is to Agatha Christie's *Mousetrap*.) The critics want to know "who done it," or at least who will have done it. Yet neither notices the dead body in the middle of the set—let alone discovers its identity—until much too late. (The set represents the drawing room of Muldoon Manor. The body lies face down on the floor, initially in front of—and intermittently under—a movable sofa.) The mystery actors are equally oblivious, eventually concluding that the body is someone named William McCoy. In fact, the real McCoy is someone named Higgs, a critic for whom Moon is a mere stand-in. Higgs has been killed by Puckeridge, Moon's own stand-in, who, unbeknownst to both Moon and Birdboot (improbably deceived by a false mustache), has been acting as Lord Muldoon, who's been acting as the real Inspector Hound, who's been posing as Major Magnus, Muldoon's half-brother. When Birdboot, in character as Simon Gascoyne, finally recognizes Higgs (now face up), Puckeridge, still in character as Magnus, kills him. (The actors then conclude, of course, that this body is Gascoyne.) When Moon, in character as the second of two false Hounds (the first having taken Moon's seat), finally recognizes Puckeridge (now minus the mustache), Puckeridge, still in character as Hound, kills him. One irony is that as both the play and the mystery-within-the-play come to an end, the only reason (or at least the real reason) the real investigator can be said to have learned "who done it" is that, having done it himself, he—or at least the critic playing him—has known all along. Another irony is that the true investigator—Stoppard's stand-in as well as ours—turns out to be Moon, once the man drops the mask. For it is Moon himself who, just after making utter nonsense of the mystery while posing as the second false Hound, or rather as Hound's stand-in's stand-in (nonsense that Puckeridge, posing as Magnus, correctly identifies as a "fantastic and implausible tale"), manages to make sense of the play by correctly identifying Puckeridge as the murderer (*Plays,* 1:43). Or at least as much sense as is humanly possible. To continue quoting that Puckeridge, there may still be "something else, something quite unknown to us, behind all this" (43). What that something is may concern the fact that murder isn't the only mystery in *The Real Inspector Hound.* Has Gascoyne really made love to Felicity Cunningham? Has he made love to Lady Muldoon? Has Birdboot made love to the actress playing Felicity? These are questions—either trivial or serious—God alone could answer.

There's no dead body in *After Magritte* (1970), Stoppard's second Agatha Christie pastiche. Nor does the mystery concern either murder or sex. It concerns both the unreliability of witnesses and the significance of seemingly "bizarre" spectacles (*Plays,* 1:58). Stoppard has described his inspiration:

> I went to see a man who had peacocks. They tend to run away.
> He was shaving one morning and he looked out the window
> and saw a peacock leap over the hedge into the road. Expensive
> animals, peacocks, so he threw down his razor and ran out and
> caught his peacock and brought it back home. I had been look-
> ing for a short piece and I had some vague idea of what I wanted
> to do. I didn't write about the man or the peacock but about two
> people who [drive] by, and, boom, they see this man in pajamas,
> with bare feet, shaving foam on his face, carrying a peacock.
> They see this man for five-eighths of a second—and that's what
> I write about. (Quoted in Gussow, 7)

But the description is inaccurate. What we're told the characters have seen before the play begins—as we but not they come to realize—may have been a barefoot man in pajamas and with shaving cream on his face (Inspector Foot), but he was holding his wife's alligator handbag, not a peacock. He was also holding a broken umbrella, wearing sunglasses, and hopping about with both feet in one pant leg. (Thanks to Foot's final monologue, we also realize how he'd come to be that way.) Thelma remains convinced she saw a young one-legged football player with shaving cream on his face, dressed in uniform, holding a ball and a cane, and hopping. Her husband, Harris, is convinced he saw "an old [blind] man with one leg and a white beard, dressed in pajamas, hopping along in the rain with a tortoise under his arm, and brandishing a white stick to clear the path through those gifted with sight" (*Plays,* 1:55). His mother ("Mother") is convinced she saw a man dressed in "the loose-fitting striped gabardine of a convicted felon," playing hopscotch, holding a handbag, wearing sunglasses and a surgical mask, and waving at her with a cricket bat (67). Another nameless woman, never on stage, is convinced she saw a one-legged minstrel holding a broken crutch and a "crocodile boot" (64). This spectacle corresponds to ones witnessed by both Constable Holmes and the audience at the beginning and end of the play. The opening spectacle, reported (or misreported) by Holmes to Foot, is of Mother asleep on an ironing board, covered by a bath towel, wearing a black bathing cap, with a bowler hat on her stomach, and of Thelma and Harris in equally odd positions. As a detective, however, Holmes is no Sherlock: That spectacle is precipitated by actions we infer but he doesn't. Nor is Foot, who fails to deduce that it was Foot himself the four saw in the street; who, based on Holmes's possibly false report, accuses Harris of having "performed without anaesthetic an illegal operation on a bald nigger minstrel about five-foot-two or Pakistani"; and who, even after he recognizes the falsity of the accusation, never realizes how they'd come to be that way (62). Foot's curtain line—the sole caption for the closing and rather crowded spectacle—is, "Well, Constable, I think you owe us all an explanation" (72). That spectacle, precipitated by actions we see but Holmes doesn't, involves a low bench-type table, about eight feet long and placed center stage. It is of Harris standing on one foot on the table, wearing a ball gown, head covered by a cushion cover, arms outstretched, and counting; of Foot—barefoot—standing next to Harris on the table, wearing sunglasses, and eating a banana; and of Mother standing on one foot on a chair placed next to Foot on the table, wearing a sock on one hand, and playing the tuba. The figures there, moreover, are punctuated by a fruit basket and a lamp shade. Thelma is in undergarments, crawling around the table, scanning the floor, and sniffing. For Holmes, who quite understandably "recoils into paralysis," it must be Foot who owes an explanation (72).

Ironically enough, as in *The Real Inspector Hound,* laymen turn out to be better investigators than lawmen. Whereas Foot's reconstruction of the preplay spectacle—a reconstruction, moreover, of his own recent past—proves "false in every particular" (much like his interpretation of the opening spectacle reported by Holmes), Thelma, Harris, and Mother get several details right (70). Thelma recalls Foot's hopping and the shaving cream, Harris his hopping and the pajamas, Mother his hopping, his sunglasses, and the handbag. Other ironies concern the nameless tortoise for which Harris mistook Foot's wife's apparently handle-free—not to mention capacious—handbag. (With handles, it couldn't have been mistaken for a ball.) As the first and least articulated of several such long-lived creatures in Stoppard, it's far more significant than anyone—including the playwright—could have known at the time. And to be conceived, or at any rate fantasized, in that handbag, whether it had handles or not, now seems to represent an alliance with something akin to that bench-type table—indeed, something akin to any messy desk (or even any drawer)—because stereotypically speaking, the married woman's handbag is a paraphernalia repository. It, too, accumulates property whose importance other people, husbands in particular, are apt to overlook. Overlook, that is, in the sense of fail to see.

The mystery in *Dirty Linen* (1976) does concern sex. But the nominal investigators are politicians, not policemen: the House of Commons Select Committee on Moral Standards in Public Life. The committee meets in a tower, which, ironically enough, does afford a ceiling view of the situation at hand—or at least a partial such view. More specifically, it meets in a room containing a conference table for the committee and a desk "with good slammable drawers" for Maddie Gotobed, their somewhat incompetent secretary (*Plays,* 1:79). Otherwise up to speed, Maddie doesn't take dictation well.

The situation is this: Some "mystery woman," to use her tabloid moniker, has been sleeping with more than a hundred members of Parliament, including all the ones on stage (84). "Someone is going through the ranks like a lawn-mower in knickers," comments one committee member (84). "Not since Dunkirk have so many people been in the same boat—proportionately speaking," comments another (135). The situation is also that newspapers are reporting the story. The mystery woman happens to be Maddie, a secret identity the committee members would rather not know. Needless to say, they'd rather no one know. Eventually, however, Maddie identifies herself—something she's in a good position to do. Like Puckeridge, Maddie's had a ceiling view all along simply because she's the one who "done" all those people: "I was in the Coq d'Or, the Golden Ox, Box Hill, Claridges and Crockford's and the Charing Cross, the Dorchester, the Green Cockatoo, Selfridges, and the Salt Beef Bar in Rupert Street with Deborah and Douglas and Cockie and Jock," Maddie reveals in no uncertain terms.

> And with Malcolm in the Metropole and in the Mandarin, the Mirabelle, and the Star of Asia in the Goldhawk Road. I was with Freddie and Reggie and Algy and Bongo and Arthur and Cyril and Tom and Ernest and Bob and the other Bob and Pongo at the Ritz and the Red Lion, the Lobster Pot, and Simpson's in the Strand—I was at the Poule au Pot and the Coq au Vin and the Côte d'Azur and Foo Luk Fok and the Grosvenor House and Luigi's and Lacy's and the Light of India with Johnny and Jackie and Jerry and Joseph and Jimmy, and in the Berkeley, Biancis, Blooms, and Muldoons with Micky and Michael and Mike and Michelle—I was in the Connaught with William, in the Westbury with Corkie, and in the Churchill with Chalky. I was at the Duke of York, the Duke of Clarence, and the Old Duke and the King Charles and the Three Kings and the Kings Arms and the Army and Navy Salad Bar with Tony and Derek and Bertie and Plantagenet and Bingo. (115–16)

The woman is prodigious, but she does use mnemonic devices.

Unlike the committee, audience members approximate what Maddie knows long before that revelation. We do so primarily because committee members have been taking her aside and either suggesting they forget certain rendezvous or returning undergarments she then shoves in a drawer. (I'd call it a secret compartment if the playwright hadn't described the drawer as slammable and if the secretary weren't shameless. At one point, Maddie "practically sprawl[s] across the desk," showing leg as well as cleavage, while shoving knickers there [85]. It's a point at which stage furniture assembles a sex object.) We also do so because they've been shouting "Strewth!" (God's truth) every time she loses outer garments—an intermittent and accidental striptease of which the committee, preoccupied by tabloid images of scantily clad secretaries strewn across the table, including one of Maddie, remains largely oblivious. For whereas the committee members' truth concerns mere fantasy—apart from Maddie, they've never even met the tabloid secretaries—God's truth concerns both fantasy and reality. It concerns Maddie as both mystery woman and secretary but also as someone else, someone quite unknown to them, behind all that.

Just who that someone is—the woman's second secret identity—may concern the fact that Maddie teaches the committee another thing or two about herself. "And I wouldn't have bothered if I knew it was supposed to be a secret—who needs it?" she concludes the revelation (116). Maddie also teaches them about other people, journalists in particular. (She's been through those ranks too.) The committee wants a report acknowledging that "the country by and large looks to its elected representatives to set a moral standard" (84); Maddie knows it doesn't. The committee finds journalists malicious; Maddie knows they aren't. "They only write it up because of each other writing it up," she instructs. "Then they try to write it up *more* than each other—it's like a competition, you see" (105, emphasis original). Having finally absorbed these lessons, the committee jettisons its voluminous and sanctimonious draft in favor of the brief, savvy report the secretary not only suggested but even—ironically enough—appears to have dictated. In other words, Maddie's a moralist as well.[15]

---

15. "All you need," Maddie suggests, "is one paragraph saying that M.P.'s have got just as much right to enjoy themselves in their own way as anyone else, and Fleet Street can take a running jump" (*Plays,* 1:105). The report reads, "In performing the duty entrusted to them your Committee took as their guiding principle that it is the just and proper expectation of every Member of Parliament, no less than for every citizen of this country, that what they choose to do in their own time, and with whom, is between them and their conscience, provided they do not transgress the right of others or the law of the land; and that this principle is not to be sacrificed to that Fleet Street stalkinghorse masquerading as a sacred cow labeled 'The People's Right to Know.' Your Committee found no evidence or even suggestion of laws broken or harm done, and thereby concludes that its business is hereby completed" (136). Maddie's dictation occurs during an intermission.

The nominal investigators in the argument plays tend to be intellectuals: either "scholars" or "academics," depending on how oblivious—or ludicrous—they are. Stoppard respects scholarship but disdains both academia and the discourse it generates.[16] In *Jumpers* (1972), the first argument play after *Rosencrantz and Guildenstern Are Dead* (1967), the intellectual is a professor of moral philosophy named George Moore. No relation to the author of *Principia Ethica,* Moore's prototype is a historian named Bone. Bone, a character in a television play by Stoppard, finds patterns within seemingly random world events and so is a bit of a chaos theorist too. The philosopher, however, writes about God. He's also written on knowledge, "comparing knowledge in the sense of having-experience-of with knowledge in the sense of being-acquainted-with, and knowledge in the sense of inferring facts with knowledge in the sense of comprehending truths"—all of which the audience should compare with "know[ledge] in the biblical sense of *screwing*" (*Jumpers,* 36, emphasis added). We see Moore in his study, assisted by a nameless secretary (sexy but competent) and distracted by a wife (sexy but distant). Like the room in *Dirty Linen,* it contains a large desk for Moore and a small one for the secretary. We also see the wife—Dorothy—in her bedroom, having a nervous breakdown. The two rooms are divided by a hallway and contained within a luxury penthouse. Note the separation, if not the elevation.

Stoppard both approves and disapproves of Moore, characterizing him as a scholar but satirizing him as an academic. He applauds the philosopher's faith in God. He endorses his absolutism, as opposed to the relativism of Vice-Chancellor Archibald Jumper. The playwright even assigns Moore some of his own protocols: his system for preparing lectures "is to scrawl them over many pieces of paper, which he then dictates to the secretary who will type them out" (23). Yet Stoppard both disorders Moore's desk ("a clutter of books and manuscripts" [14]), thereby indicating a disordered mind, and deplores the man's obliviousness of two facts concerning sex and murder: that Jumper both "screws" Dorothy and shoots a colleague named McFee. The body's in the bedroom. Moore,

---

16. See Gussow, 53, where Stoppard reminds the interviewer he's "not an academic."

moreover, is oblivious of the fact that Dorothy, mentally shattered, needs his help. A stage direction puts it neatly: The husband has an "uncomprehending heart" (41). Thus, to quote academic discourse, "on one side there is an image of the scholar in the ivory tower, ruminating over philosophy in an abstract, theoretical way, while on the other side there is a tangible embodiment of the ethical issues that form the core of George's philosophical quest" (Fleming, 86). McFee—as visible as Higgs yet invisible to Moore—represents one such embodiment. Stoppard's moral, in other words: Practice what you teach.

As does *After Magritte,* the play opens with a bizarre spectacle. This one includes both Jumper shooting McFee and the secretary performing a striptease while swinging from a chandelier. (Note the elevation.) These actions, we come to understand, represent a party Dorothy gave the night before. Later in act 1, Inspector Bones (not Bone) arrives to find Moore holding a bow and arrow in one hand and a tortoise in the other, his face covered in shaving cream. The pet's named Pat. We understand this spectacle too, but the policeman quite understandably recoils into paralysis. Bones, moreover, is a bit of a Foot. (He even has family named Foot.) Relatively clueless, he infers that Dorothy killed McFee— as does Moore. Dorothy alone suspects Jumper. Act 2 ends with George standing on his desk, stomping on Pat, and holding Thumper, the pet hare he's also killed by accident. (The allusion is to Aesop.) Given what we know about Moore, it's a variation on Maddie sprawled across the furniture. Given what we know about the playwright, all three spectacles indicate Stoppard's Bone-like fondness of finding order within the chaos of personal history. As Stoppard himself explained at the time, "The only way I really work is to assemble a strange pig's breakfast of visual images and thoughts and try to shake them into some kind of coherent pattern" (quoted in Gussow, 18). The meal metaphor may have occurred to Stoppard in that kitchen of his.

Jumper, of course, knows more about the sex and murder than either Bones or Moore. Like Puckeridge and Maddie, he's the one who done 'em. But there are two figures on stage that may know more than Jumper—witnesses who, unlike the ones in *After Magritte,* don't say anything and so aren't necessarily unreliable.

In fact, they're both mute and inscrutable. Has the secretary seen Jumper shoot McFee, among other spectacles? We'll never know. She never speaks. She's "poker-faced" (14). Even when she nods at Jumper we're told it's "impossible to draw any conclusions" (56). And so the woman nearly represents the writer's God: a desk-bound—and ceiling-suspended—observer who could teach a thing or two but, unlike Maddie, doesn't. (She's no moralist.) Only she's too unaware of her own situation to qualify for that job: The poor woman failed to see that her dead fiancé—McFee—was an adulterer. "His wife knew about *her*," reports an Alfred Doolittle avatar, "but *she* didn't know about his wife" (80, emphasis original). (As an audience member, Stoppard tends to watch the secretary—possibly because he alone knows her grief.) Nor will we ever know what Pat saw. For a slowpoke, he certainly gets around—or rather gets left around the apartment by his fond but forgetful owner: first of all in the bedroom, last of all on that desk ("Crrrrrunch!!!" [81]). This suggests he's a tortoise for reasons unrelated to paraphernalia. Like the Mock Turtle's beloved master (not to mention the playwright himself), it's easy to imagine Moore's pet—likewise granted speech—having "taught us" a thing or two involving both inference and comprehension. Or, granted a comprehending heart, both intellect and emotion.

Like *After Magritte, Travesties* (1974) concerns the unreliability of witnesses. It also concerns self-examination. Or rather, situating oneself in history. The witness—and self-examiner—is Henry Carr, a man who really did cross paths with Joyce during the First World War. That Carr, no intellectual, starred in his Zurich production of *The Importance of Being Earnest*. He also played a minor role at the British consulate there. Stoppard's Carr is a demented, self-aggrandizing old man who imagines he also met both Lenin and Tristan Tzara. (Of the three, he considers Joyce "an amazing intellect" and Lenin an "intellectual theoretician" [*Travesties*, 22, 23]. Like Dadaism in general, Tzara warrants no such validation.) And who's to say he didn't meet them? Stoppard's play is under Carr's control, and so no other character approaches a ceiling view. At least, not until his wife steps in at the end to correct him. "You never even saw Lenin," she tells him. "And you were never the Consul." "Oh, Cecily," he replies, "I wish I'd known then that you'd turn out to be a pedant!" (98). Stoppard, of course, controls *Travesties* too. Like "Oxen of the Sun" in *Ulysses* (for Carr, *Elasticated Bloomers*), *Travesties* is "a minor anthology of styles-of-play, styles-of-language," including Wildean pastiche, Joycean pastiche, Shavian dialectics, and limericks (quoted in Marowitz, 5).[17] So consider it Irish, but Stoppard himself Czech. A bounced Czech.[18]

The play opens with Joyce, Lenin, and Tzara working at desks in the Zurich Public Library. Tzara is writing random English words on a sheet of paper he then snips word by word into his hat. (Bishop's Harvard students, you'll recall, did sestinas this way.) Oddly enough, the poem he pulls out makes sense—in French. ("Eel ate enormous appletzara / key dairy chef's hat he'll learn oomparah! / Ill raced alas whispers kill later nut east, / noon avuncular ill day Clara!" [*Travesties*, 18].) Lenin, assisted by Cecily, the librarian, is writing on imperialism. Joyce is dictating "Oxen of the Sun" to Carr's sister Gwendolyn, who will type it out. (The protocols, of course, are Stoppard's. The women's names are taken from *Earnest*.) All three men are occupied with books, papers, pencils, and (in Tzara's case) scissors, but they fail to assemble significant objects, let alone sex objects. Cecily, however, works at a reference desk that keeps becoming a platform. She stands on it to deliver a lecture on Marx while removing her clothes. Whereas her (political) focus is communist revolution, Carr's focus (personal and sex-crazed) is Cecily, his future wife—which explains the striptease. Then Lenin stands on it to lecture on Marx. His focus is literature—or rather, totalitarian control thereof. Note

---

17. To quote Stoppard's Joyce: "An impromptu poet of Hibernia / rhymed himself into a hernia. / He became quite adept / at the practice except / for occasional anti-climaxes" (*Travesties*, 35). I write limericks too, including ones on modernists. On Wilde: "While posing above an abyss, / poor Oscar said something amiss— / a damnably glib / sodomitical fib: / 'The boy was too ugly to kiss.'" On Nijinsky: "Most audience members cried 'Shame!' / when Vaslav, Diaghilev's flame, / defiled the veil / in a pastoral tale. / But wankers were happy they came." On Rorem: "Atonal is straight, tonal gay, / claim students of Miss Boulanger. / Take little Ned: / even in bed / he'd carry a tune all the way." On Marais: "All those who love stunners with smarts— / if not in real life, in the arts— / should go to a show / by surreal Cocteau. / The guy gave Jean all the best parts."

18. Tomás Sträussler was born in Czechoslovakia on July 3, 1937. His parents fled the country less than two years later, but it wasn't until 1994 that the playwright learned both of them were Jewish. I will refrain from further comment on the irony of this ignorance.

the underscoring of Stoppard's desk/stage analogy. Note too the characters' elevation. But they're still figments of Carr's imagination. They still couldn't know more than he.

You will have observed an abundance of ecdysiasts in Stoppard. Although not above titillating an audience, the playwright is more interested in stripping as a metaphor for truth revelation.[19] Maddie, for example, reveals her secret identity and Cecily her desirability, both relatively uncomplicated matters. But it's not a good metaphor for Carr's Proustian quest. (Or pseudo-Proustian: Carr's creator can't finish *À la recherche.* "I took it on holiday once and got through one and a half volumes," Stoppard admits; "[t]he holiday ended and that was the end of Proust" [quoted in Gussow, 52].) He really wants to know the truth of his own distant past as well as the related truth of his present subjectivity. These truths, Stoppard suggests, are complicated matters God alone masters, and so the play itself, to quote another academic, is also "a model of the indirections by which we must move toward the white light of a truth beyond our full perception or expression" (Whitaker, 114). These indirections may include senile dementia, as in Carr's case, but they necessarily include linguistic mediation: styles-of-play, styles-of-language. And none of us—demented or not—ever avoids the kind of mediation involved when Carr keeps seeing himself as Algernon Moncrieff, the role he played in *Earnest.*

By linguistic, I mean ideological—even if Stoppard wouldn't. Just as Ernest Worthing, Algernon's friend and older brother, is another name for John, mediation is another word for what Althusser, citing Lacan, calls misrecognition. And none of us avoids the kind of misrecognition involved when subjecting ourselves to discursive forms inevitably controlled by historical forces—including forms, like *Earnest* and *Ulysses,* labeled literary. In other words, mastering impressive precursors—not to mention anthologizing them—also represents ideological subjection. This, I take it, is the unintended point of Lenin's lecture.

Stoppard's moral: Know thyself. This, of course, is pure Socrates: a motto inscribed above his academy—and desk, according to sources ignorant of both furniture history and the fact that

---

19. See Barthes, *Pleasure of the Text,* 10: "To denude [is] to know, to learn the origin and the end."

the man never wrote anything. (Given the end of that story, "Kill thyself" may have been more like it. Stoppard claims to want "No symbolism admitted and none denied" inscribed at the entrance to his study.) Or not so pure: Socrates got the phrase from the Delphic oracle. But truly knowing ourselves as subjects of history is no more possible than knowing ourselves as Athenians would have been—in part because there's too much to know (history is chaotic), in part because we lack sufficient critical distance. We're never not text, never outside ideology.[20] This isn't to say we shouldn't keep trying, dialectically. Nor does Stoppard—or (Plato's) Socrates—ever say we shouldn't. Both see self-examination as an endless process.

Knowing someone else, of course, is equally endless, although it can appear to take no time at all. *The Real Thing* (1982) features a witty, intellectual playwright who, like Stoppard, loves pop music and semipublic work space. He also loves his wife. When we first encounter the newlyweds at home—Henry writing at a makeshift and relatively bare desk in their living room with the radio on low, Annie distracting him—he's completely smitten. Too smitten, in fact, to see her clearly. In other words, he's still idealizing or, in Stendhalian terms, "crystallizing" her. But when we last encounter them less than three years later—Annie getting ready for bed, Henry turning up the volume on "I'm a Believer"—he may see her as really she is. (Henry's makeshift desk, which does have drawers, corresponds to a theatrical stage. His final desk corresponds to a cinematic screen because he's gone Hollywood for additional income. Apart from the radio, it contains a television, video monitor, and typewriter.)

In other words, having both investigated and discovered in the interim what it means to have a comprehending heart, Henry now loves Annie, as Marguerite Yourcenar would have it, with open eyes—and more or less as a friend. (According to Yourcenar, love requires "a feeling for the other person's freedom and dignity coupled with clear-sighted acceptance of that person as he or she

---

20. Cf. Bull, 150: Stoppard's political credo, made clearest in *Arcadia*, is "that the individual is more . . . than just a construction of the political state; that all ideologies will crumble in the face of individual will; but that the result is not an ungovernable chaos, [it is] rather a set of unpredictable patterns."

really is" [254]. Unlike Moore in *Jumpers,* Henry has accepted his wife "at her worst" [*Plays,* 5:224].)[21] And sex has nothing to do with it, notwithstanding what Henry used to believe. For the playwright's playwright, words defy "incomprehension" (5:207). (They defy "chaos" too, unlike some of Henry's conduct. "I don't believe in behaving well," he tells Annie at a crisis point. "I believe in mess, tears, pain, self-abasement, loss of self-respect, nakedness" [5:207, 231].) For the old Henry, intercourse defies incomprehension as well. "It's to do with knowing and being known," he tells his teenage daughter Debbie—although she asked about love. (Unlike Maddie's men, Henry mustn't fantasize.)

> I remember how it stopped seeming odd that in biblical Greek knowing was used for making love. Whosit knew so-and-so. Carnal knowledge. It's what lovers trust each other with. Knowledge of each other, not of the flesh but through the flesh, knowledge of self, the real him, the real her, *in extremis,* the mask slipped from the face. Every other version of oneself is on offer to the public. We share our vivacity, grief, sulks, anger, joy . . . we hand it out to anybody who happens to be standing around, to friends and family with a momentary sense of indecency perhaps, to strangers without hesitation. Our lovers share us with the passing trade. But in pairs we insist that we give ourselves to each other. What selves? What's left? What else is there that hasn't been dealt out like a pack of cards? A sort of knowledge. Personal, final, uncompromised. Knowing, being known. I revere that. (5:220, ellipsis original)[22]

---

21. There are, of course, other conceptions of love. Wilde, for one, believes in linguistic mediation. "Do you wish to love?" he asks: "Use Love's Litany, and the words will create the yearning from which the world fancies that they spring" (399). Auden, for another, "maintains" Stendhalian crystallization. "When someone begins to lose the glamour they had for us on our first meeting them, we tell ourselves that we have been deceived, that our fantasy cast a halo over them which they are unworthy to bear," he told himself at the end of one love affair. "It is always possible however that the reverse is the case; that our disappointment is due to a failure of our own sensibility which lacks the strength to maintain itself at the acuteness with which it began. People may really be what we first thought them, and what we subsequently think of as the disappointing reality, the person obscured by the staleness of our senses." Cf. Adorno 79: "Once wholly a possession, the loved person is no longer really looked at."

22. "Know thyself." Does this dictum, then, by combining Hebraism and Hellenism, suggest self-examination as masturbation? Masturbation as self-examination?

Unfortunately, he can't write plays that way—which is to say, he can't write about love. What Henry can write (apart from dramas telling Sartre where he, Sartre, "got it wrong"—an allusion to *Rosencrantz and Guildenstern Are Dead*) are derivative comedies that he thinks concern both love and "self-knowledge through pain" but that are really about, well, screwing—or as Debbie puts it, "did she have it off or didn't she?" (5:156, 218). (His current production, *The House of Cards,* resembles Noël Coward. Where sex is concerned, it also resembles *The Real Inspector Hound.*)[23] It so happens she didn't, just as Annie—even at her worst—doesn't have sex with an actor named Billy. But for Debbie, as for both Annie and Stoppard, the question—or mystery—is trivial, the answer not worth knowing. So who *cares* if Simon Gascoyne screwed Felicity Cunningham? Or Lady Muldoon. Or even if Birdboot screwed the actress playing Felicity. For that matter, who cares if Jumper screwed Dorothy?[24]

Henry, of course, can't see Annie as she really is no matter how long he loves her. He'll see more and more of her if he's attentive—even, perhaps, as a widower. But he'll only ever approximate that ceiling view, in part because she'll keep changing, in part because she may not know herself that well, in part because no memory is "indifferent to the future of him who harbors it" (Adorno, 166). Nor is Henry alone. All beloveds remain beyond our—and their—full perception or expression.

Take Flora Crewe, the heroine of *Indian Ink* (1995). (My chronology may seem off, but *Indian Ink* is based on a 1991 radio play.) Flora is the first of three dead poets with whom Stoppard concerns himself, but the only fictional one. The others are Byron in *Arcadia* and A. E. Housman in *The Invention of Love.* I exclude Tzara and Joyce. Like Maddie, another underestimated sex object, Flora is a promiscuous young British woman. She tends to versify

---

23. *The Real Thing* opens by presenting *The House of Cards* as if *it* were the real thing. Only later do we learn it's a play within the play. We're not that duped by the play presumably called *The Real Inspector Hound* within *The Real Inspector Hound.*
24. For Debbie, making "such a crisis" of marital infidelity is what comes of making "such a mystery" of sex (5:218–19). For Annie, asking about infidelity isn't caring. "If I had an affair," she tells Henry, "it would be out of need. Care about that" (5:231). Stoppard both clarifies and qualifies his indifference in *Indian Ink.*

sex as well because, as she puts it when accused of obscenity, you should "write what you know" (*Plays,* 5:441). Yet she's capable of love, as well as of inspiring it—even beyond the grave. (Flora dies of tuberculosis while visiting India in 1930.) Her latest admirer is Eldon Pike, an obsessed, oblivious, and footnote-spouting English professor (American, of course, and fictional) who, having edited Flora's poems and correspondence, is now, at some point in the 1980s, writing her biography—a book sure to "get her wrong" (5:373).[25] (Like *Arcadia* and *The Invention of Love, Indian Ink* is set in two time periods: historical past and dramatic present. It's no postcolonial critique, however.)[26] Pike is the first of three literary critics with whom Stoppard concerns himself. The others are Housman and both Hannah Jarvis and Bernard Nightingale (also fictional, but British) in *Arcadia.* Like Pike, Nightingale's an academic; Hannah and Housman, scholars.

Flora is a composite figure representing both the beloved and the playwright himself—those two people Stoppard finds most worth knowing. As with Annie, he created the character for actress Felicity Kendal, his partner at the time. As with Henry, Flora shares some of Stoppard's protocols: using a fountain pen, reading work in progress aloud, and writing both poetry and correspondence on a table in a semipublic work space, the verandah of her bungalow in Jummapur. Stoppard, moreover, composed reams of her poetry (not correspondence) prior to the play. Pike is singular, not to mention single-minded. For one thing, all this investigator really wants to know is whether the poet was painted nude, if so by whom, and whether the work—one *we* know to be a watercolor—exists anymore. His sole clue is a letter Flora wrote to

---

25. See *Plays,* 5:471: Pike advises his Indian—and less dim-witted—research assistant that "all we want is the facts and to tell the truth in our fashion." See also Fleming, 212: *Indian Ink* concerns "the difficulties and fallibility involved in trying to reconstruct the past." Stoppard's attitude to literary biography is self-contradictory: He does appreciate Richard Ellmann's work on both Joyce and Wilde.

26. Stoppard lived in India as a child, which may account for his nostalgic and orientalizing treatment of the place. Although the play ends by quoting Emily Eden in *Up the Country* (1866)—"I sometimes wonder they do not cut all our heads off and say nothing more about it"—at least one character situates Eden as yet another figure in Wonderland: not the Mock Turtle but the decapitation-crazed Queen of Hearts (*Plays,* 5:482). Cf. Lee and Zinman.

Eleanor Swan, her younger and still grief-stricken sister. The letter contains the line "Perhaps my soul will stay behind as a smudge of paint on paper, as if I'd always been here, like Radha who was the most beautiful of the herdswomen, undressed for love in an empty house" (5:480). Pike has no interest in whether Flora actually posed for such a portrait, in what her posing nude would have meant, in what her *not* posing would have meant, nor in her personal relations, if any, with the artist. (Compare his attitude—and Eleanor's—to that of Cassandra Millar, the Disch character who reads Proust to approximate an understanding of death.)

Flora was, in fact, painted nude by a young man named Nirad Das—information Pike, despite his intellectual limitations, both intuits and confirms. (Ironically, the far less dim-witted Nightingale is far more off base about Byron.) The work, moreover, still exists. It hasn't been hidden in plain sight, however—hung on some wall or displayed on some table. It's been locked away in a trunk Das left to his son Anish—a drawer-like secret compartment indicative of the artist's interiority—and only now is it displayed by the son on the sister's garden table, which also happens to be where Pike read that letter. (Meanwhile, Eleanor has been keeping a relatively modest oil portrait of Flora by an "unknown Indian artist" stashed away on top of a wardrobe and then in a cupboard [5:385]. Pike reproduced that portrait in his edition of the correspondence; Anish Das, having recognized the reproduction as his father's work, also discovered the identity of his mysterious nude. He and Eleanor resolve to keep the existence of the watercolor from both Pike and, by implication, the public—for the artist's sake, not the poet's.) Nirad Das, of course, knew all this as well as the nature of his relations with Flora. If still alive, he'd be the play's Puckeridge. Anish Das, recognizing a certain symbolism in the watercolor (a dying vine embracing a dark tree trunk) suspects—correctly—that they were sexually involved. (Another symbol speaks to Eleanor: "An open book on the bed, that's Flora" [5:448]. By way of ironic contrast, an old Rajasthani painting of Radha given to Flora by some rajah—another erotic watercolor—and then concealed in a book given to her by Nirad Das [Emily Eden's *Up the Country*] may still be there. Eleanor, who inherited the book, gives it back to his son. God knows if she or anyone else ever removed that nude. The closed book, moreover, corresponds to the locked trunk, just as the watercolors correspond.) But Anish Das gets the order wrong: The nude painting session came before the intercourse and not, as the young man would have it, the other way around. Flora, moreover, never posed nude for Nirad Das. He did that work from memory, imagination, and maybe even fantasy, the poet having performed an inadvertent striptease for the painter prior to that session, when he happened to see her taking a bath. "It's too late for modesty," Flora remarked at the time (5:423). Eleanor mistakenly thinks the two didn't have sex and—even more mistakenly—also thinks it wouldn't have mattered if they had. Like Debbie, but unlike Stoppard now, she considers any such truth not worth knowing. "It hardly matters, looking back. Men were not really important to Flora. If they had been, they would have been fewer. She used them like batteries. When things went flat, she'd put in a new one" (5:476).

Some of us, of course, know the two had sex. As mentioned earlier, in a footnote, directors confirm the fact by having her wear his clothing the morning after. The audience is also privileged to know that Flora—like Stoppard—sees stripping as truth revelation, either as an artist's model or as one's mistress. ("Am I to lay myself bare before you?" Flora teases Nirad Das early on [5:381].) Naked before a partner, she may consider herself known in the biblical sense—if, that is, undressed for love and not just sex. To quote the poem she writes while Nirad Das does the oil painting:

> Yes I am in heat like a bride in a bath
> without secrets, soaked in heated air
> that liquifies to the touch and floods,
> shortening the breath, yes
> I am discovered, heat has found me out. (5:380)

Nude before a painter, Flora feels the work produced may be more emotionally honest than otherwise. (She'd also stripped for Modigliani.) It may have more *rasa,* Sanskrit for the nine moods artwork should evoke: fear, disgust, anger, humor, wonder, compassion, heroism, tranquility, and—as here—"erotic love" (5:408). Hence the "soul" revealed to—and by—Nirad Das in the stripping,

the nude painting, and then the lovemaking (the one to "stay behind as a smudge of paint on paper") is that of a relatively immodest
person not averse to screwing for the fun of it but also not averse to
amorous engagement when the right partner presents himself; in
this case, a sexy guy who happens to be "a friend and fellow artist" as
well (5:388). (Yourcenar would be pleased.) The soul is also that of
a relatively shameless, Maddie-like person who doesn't care what
strangers think about her, even if they believe lies. "Report what
you like," Flora tells David Durance, another oblivious investigator
who's crystallized her. "I don't mind, you see" (5:475). (Stendhal
would be pleased—with Durance.) This is why Eleanor is quite
mistaken in claiming "it hardly matters." That unknown Indian
painter was one man who didn't underestimate Flora. Having both
seen and loved her with open eyes, Nirad Das could represent her
more or less as she was at the time and then, without fantasizing,
truly "know" her that way.[27]

Like Carr's subjectivity, Flora's truth—that "soul" of hers—is
far more complicated than either Maddie's secret identity or
Cecily's desirability. And of course, there's even more to her than
that. For one thing, the poet doesn't see desks the way the playwright does. To the poet, they're simply inanimate objects. When
Flora asked Modigliani to show her the now nonexistent nude he
was doing of her, he asked, "Why? When I paint a table I don't
have to show it to the table" (5:393). Shortly after that bath,
she tells Nirad Das, "When I was Modi's model I might as well
have *been* a table. When he was done, he got rid of me" (5:429,
emphasis original). (I presume Modigliani screwed her before the
sitting, not after. I also presume his painting had no *rasa* because
although Flora considered herself a friend, Modigliani didn't.)[28]
But like any beloved—or self—Flora remains beyond one's full
perception or expression. Or as Nirad Das puts it, "The truth will

27. The Flora Crewe/Nirad Das relationship resembles that of Adela Quested and
Dr. Aziz in Forster's *A Passage to India,* and they both seem to know it. Part of both
Forster's and Stoppard's erotic fantasies of South Asia, moreover, may be that the
differences between love and lust and between sexual love and nonsexual friendship
don't make much difference there.

28. *Plays,* 5:394: "He painted his friends clothed," Flora tells Nirad Das. "For nudes he
used models. I believe I was his friend. But perhaps not. Perhaps a used model only."

never be known, only to God who is merciful" (5:404). He means Krishna—a god with whom the painter himself is closely but not absolutely identified. (Better Krishna than Puckeridge.) Krishna, we're told, is Radha's beloved, just as Nirad Das is Flora's. ("I wasn't sure whether Krishna was a god or a person," Flora asks. "Oh, he was most certainly a god," Nirad Das replies, "one of the ten incarnations of Vishnu, and a favorite subject of the old Rajasthani painters. He had a great love affair, you see, with a married lady, Radha, who was the most beautiful of the herdswomen. Radha fell passionately in love with Krishna and she would often escape from her husband to meet him in secret" [5:405].) And unlike Durance, who is only slightly elevated when—on horseback—he falls in love at first sight, Nirad Das also approximates the omniscient god's ceiling view when he first sees Flora. The poet was speaking on "Literary Life in London" at the Jummapur Theosophical Society. The painter, in attendance because fond of British writing (Agatha Christie in particular), was sitting almost directly above her. Or as Flora describes the scene in another, earlier letter to Eleanor: "My lecture drew a packed house . . . and a much more sensible house than mine, built round a courtyard with a flat roof all round so I had an audience in the gods like gods in the audience" (5:373).

The house in *Arcadia* (1993) is a stately home. We see, or rather imagine, it both as it was in the early 1800s, standing in a typical English park of the time, and in its present form. All we really see is a room on the garden front. This room looks relatively bare despite the large table that occupies its center. This table accumulates objects of which Hannah Jarvis and Bernard Nightingale are more or less oblivious despite their correlation to truths these two intellectuals strive to discover. To quote Stoppard: "During the course of the play the table collects this and that, and where an object from one scene would be an anachronism in another . . . it is simply deemed to have become invisible" (*Arcadia*, 15). By the end of the play, it's "a considerable mess of papers, books, and objects" (92–93).[29]

---

29. Stoppard, *Arcadia*, 15: "In the case of props," the playwright understates, "there is no absolute need to remove the evidence of one period to make way for another."

Jarvis, an independent scholar, is there to research the history of the garden, which by 1810 contained a hermitage.[30] Like Stoppard, the woman is a classicist with a mania for order. "There's an engraving of Sidley Park in 1730 that makes you want to weep," she tells Nightingale:

> Paradise in the age of reason. By 1760 everything had gone—the topiary, pools and terraces, fountains, an avenue of limes—the whole sublime geometry was ploughed under by Capability Brown. The grass went from the doorstep to the horizon and the best box hedge in Derbyshire was dug up for the ha-ha so that the fools could pretend they were living in God's countryside. And then Richard Noakes came in to bring God up to date. (27)[31]

She's most interested in who the presumably demented hermit was and what he was doing there. An 1832 travel guide indicating Noakes's "horrid" style specifies "a hermitage occupied by a lunatic since twenty years without discourse or companion save for a pet tortoise, Plautus by name, which he suffers children to touch upon request" (64). A contemporaneous letter from Thomas Love Peacock calls the hermit "a savant among idiots, a sage of lunacy"

---

30. Prompted perhaps by Nightingale's nasty description of her book on Carolyn Lamb as a "novelette" (*Arcadia,* 59), Stoppard biographer Ira Nadel misidentifies Jarvis as a "novelist" (Nadel, viii, 426, 443). Unlike Pike, however, he doesn't seem to get anything else wrong. See Barthes, *Mythologies,* 65, and Bachelard, 31, on "hut dreams." See also my discussion of Bishop's "The End of March" in "Desk Work." For Stoppard's own hut dream, see Gussow, 135: "My version of retirement is to be a poet, by which I don't mean that I want to stop work, because I love work, but my ideal form of retirement would be to spend six months on a poem, which I then wouldn't have to show anybody." Unlike Bishop, this writer's still writing, not to mention working at a (for him) more difficult genre than drama—and, now that his work space is completely private, doing so with no audience in mind.

31. Noakes, a fictional character, imposed romantic "sublimity" on Brown's picturesque scheme. The ha-ha, a trench, was used as part of such schemes both to create visual continuity between stately homes and the surrounding parkland and to keep cows off the lawn. The name (pronounced *ha*-ha) derives from the supposedly pleasant surprise of finding one's way into the park suddenly blocked by a heretofore invisible barrier, as opposed to an iron fence or box hedge. Nightingale enters Sidley Park by nearly driving into one. So it's no surprise when he tries to charm Jarvis by sharing an erroneous theory of pronunciation. "Ha-*hah*, not *ha*-ha. If you were strolling down the garden and all of a sudden the ground gave way at your feet, you're not going to go '*ha*-ha,' you're going to jump back and go 'ha-*hah*!,' or more probably, 'Bloody 'ell!'" (*Arcadia,* 20, emphasis added).

(26). In Hindu mythology, the tortoise would symbolize the hermit: the one withdrawing from material distraction into spirituality, the other into its shell. I'm not sure Stoppard knows this, nor if he'd care. ("No symbolism admitted and none denied.")

Nightingale, another English professor, wants to know what Byron was doing at Sidley Park shortly before the hermitage came to be. All the poet really did was a little hunting, a little writing, and a lot of screwing. He claimed to have shot a hare, as recorded in the game book at the time. In fact it was shot by Augustus Coverly, the next Lord Croom. (Heir kills hare.) He seems to have panned poetry by Ezra Chater, another house guest. In fact, the anonymous notice in the *Piccadilly Recreation* was penned by Septimus Hodge, a classmate of Byron's employed by Lady Croom to instruct Thomasina Coverly. (Not for long, though: Thomasina burns to death at sixteen.) Byron, however, did add a few derogatory lines about Chater's *Couch of Eros* to Lady Croom's copy of *English Bards and Scotch Reviewers*. And he actually managed to have sex with Mrs. Chater. (So did Hodge, but only in lieu of Lady Croom. As the clever tutor himself tells his beloved employer, "I thought in my madness that the Chater with her skirts over her head would give me the momentary illusion of the happiness to which I dared not put a face" [72].) Byron also had sex with Lady Croom. (So did Hodge. So will a certain Count Zelinsky. Like Flora, the woman is promiscuous but loving.) Nightingale discovers Byron's screwing of "the Chater" but is wrong about the hunting and writing. Convinced Byron both killed the hare and wrote the *Piccadilly* notice, he's also convinced the poet both killed Chater and then fled the country. The table, Jarvis indicates to Nightingale's horror, displays undeniable evidence to the contrary: a nineteenth-century garden book identifying and a twentieth-century flower pot containing the species Chater discovered sometime after he was supposed to be dead. Nightingale's been "fucked by a dahlia," as the academic himself puts it (88).[32]

---

32. This inspector is a bit of a Bones: Nightingale, too, treats the past as a murder mystery. Plautus, however, is a bit of a Foot: This stage name of the Roman playwright Titus Maccius means "splay-foot." I'm almost sure the tortoise symbolizes Stoppard (Straüssler). Chater anticipates Stoppard's Housman: Confusion created by the latter's double identity as both poet and scholar echoes confusion created by the former's double identity as both poet and botanist.

Nightingale, of course, considers himself a "scholar" (58). It is Jarvis who calls him an academic, in large part because the man is frequently mistaken—not to mention "arrogant, greedy, and reckless" (59). Nightingale also misconstrues how Hodge's copy of *The Couch of Eros*—concealing urgent letters from both Mr. and Mrs. Chater, much as *Up the Country* conceals the Rajasthani watercolor—came to be in Byron's possession. Lady Croom took the book for Byron, who Nightingale thinks borrowed it. Since the letters lack covers, he misconstrues them as Byron's too. And he's wrong about a drawing by Henry Fuseli entitled "Lord Byron and Carolyn Lamb at the Royal Academy." Nightingale mistakenly thinks it was done too late to be them. He does get a few things right, however—if at times for the wrong reasons or even inadvertently. Unaware of all the men having sex with Lady Croom, Nightingale correctly infers that Byron had sex with Mrs. Chater, but he does so from the concealed letters, which of course really implicate Hodge alone. And he glibly posits the existence of a "lost but ineradicable" letter confirming everything he believes—part of which is true, part of which isn't (57). Byron did send such a letter to Hodge, who burned it unread. But Nightingale must be somewhat mistaken as to its contents. Whereas that letter probably indicated the poet's sexual involvement with both women, it couldn't possibly have indicated his shooting of Chater. To his credit, however, Nightingale knows—or, rather, intuits—that Peacock's letter about the hermit was sent to Thackeray.

Jarvis isn't fucked by anything—or anyone, for that matter. (Unlike "academic" Nightingale, "scholar" Jarvis is almost never wrong. Her only erroneous conclusions, moreover, are insignificant. Like Nightingale, she credits Byron with minor publications by Hodge. She also considers a doodle by Thomasina "the only known likeness of the Sidley hermit" [25]. That drawing, done on Noakes's prospectus, is of some hypothetical occupant.) The hermit, Jarvis both intuits and confirms, was Hodge.[33] And he wasn't demented. He was devoted, both to the memory of his clever,

---

33. See Fleming, 201: Jarvis may be "a champion of the dispassionate intellect," but she relies on instinct as well. "In short, she embodies Stoppard's notion that classical and romantic temperaments are not mutually exclusive, but rather coexist in people."

prodigious student and to the proximity of her mother. Hodge, still in love with Lady Croom, wished to be near her. This, Jarvis doesn't recognize. He also needed time and space to work out one of Thomasina's two uncanny discoveries. This, Jarvis does recognize. Shortly before her premature death and long before her time in general, the girl discovers both entropy and iterated algorithms (which she calls "the New Geometry of Irregular Forms" [43])—or in other words, both the second law of thermodynamics and chaos mathematics. ("God's truth, Septimus," she tells her tutor, thereby associating chaos theory with omniscience, "if there is an equation for a curve like a bell, there must be an equation for one like a bluebell, and if a bluebell, why not a rose?" [37].) Hodge the hermit concerned himself with entropy, producing "thousands of pages" of calculations then mistaken for "cabalistic proofs that the world was coming to an end"—which of course they were, in a way (27). These, too, were burned. (A labor of love—and grief—for Thomasina; in other words, an introjection. As if to indicate our less-than-omniscient position, Stoppard leads the audience to believe the calculations were an iterated algorithm by having Valentine Coverly—a modern-day chaos mathematician as well as the current heir—find a lesson book of Thomasina's containing her New Geometry, help Jarvis see the New Geometry as an iterated algorithm, and then tell her both that another algorithm concerning grouse, which he has just spent several months doing on his computer, "would take me the rest of my life to do again [by hand]—thousands of pages" and that "you'd have to be insane" to work that way [51, 52]. Valentine would organize "messy" data contained in the Coverly game books by finding "the lost algorithm" or, in other words, the "tune" in all that "noise" [46].) The corroborative evidence on the table: the lesson book, also containing Thomasina's diagram of entropy; a portfolio containing a drawing she did of Hodge with Plautus; and, believe it or not, Plautus himself.

It is Valentine, flirting with Jarvis, who explains the diagram. Although Thomasina "didn't have the maths," he tells her, "she saw what things meant, way ahead, like seeing a picture." She saw why when you break a window, "you can put back the bits of glass but you can't collect up the heat of the smash" (93). It is

Valentine's younger brother Gus, in love with Jarvis, who knowingly brings the drawing to her attention. (Like the secretary in *Jumpers,* Gus is mute—also unaccountably so. Unlike her, he does represent the writer's God, although neither desk-bound nor ceiling-suspended. There's nothing Gus doesn't seem to know, and even Stoppard isn't sure why this "genius" won't speak [33].) And although the all-important tortoise on the table may be known as "Lightning" to both Jarvis and Valentine (his owner), the animal, Stoppard tells us, "is not readily distinguishable from Plautus" (43). Perhaps this is merely to economize. After all, play producers will find one tortoise cheaper than two. Even Hodge economizes by using Plautus as a paperweight. But I prefer to think Valentine unwittingly inherits the hermit's pet. After all, it could live that long—an accountably mute but presumably reliable witness of the historical past the two intellectuals would reclaim. (Not that Plautus/Lightning gets around as much as Pat. Nor does he need to. All the significant action in Sidley Park seems to occur in the garden room and then the hermitage. In other words, that mountain of evidence always comes to this Mohammed.) As such, Plautus/Lightning resembles Chater, that poet/botanist mistaken by Nightingale for two different people. He also resembles that purloined letter: another smoking gun, as it were, hidden in plain sight. (Lightning enters *Arcadia* "half-hidden on the table" [18].) He also resembles a rather sharp twentieth-, now twenty-first-century audience member who both catches and recalls not so much Stoppard's allusions as all the nineteenth-century information.[34]

---

34. This information includes the facts that Augustus shot Byron's hare, that Fuseli drew Byron, and that the poet sent Hodge a letter confirming everything. The audience also enjoys a nearly omniscient sense of ironic repetitions. Lady Croom responds "I *do not* know when *I have* received a more unusual compliment" to Hodge's remark about "the Chater" with skirts over her head; Jarvis responds "I *don't* know when *I've* received a more unusual proposal" to Valentine's flirtatious remark about having a trial marriage and then calling it off in the morning (*Arcadia,* 72, 75, emphasis added). (Note the contractions.) Thomasina, wondering if God is a Newtonian, asks Hodge if she's "the first person *to think* of this"; eighteen-year-old Chloë Coverly, wondering if the only thing wrong in Newton's universe "is people fancying people who aren't part of the plan," asks Valentine if *she's* "the first person *to have thought* of this" (5, 73, emphasis added). (Note the expansion.) They're both first. Another ironic repetition we may recognize—God certainly would—is that Chloë's crush on Nightingale replicates Thomasina's on Hodge. Yet Nightingale screws Chloë, whereas Hodge never makes love to Thomasina.

In other words, the tortoise—like the table he's staged upon—represents dramatic irony. He even resembles an *immortal,* omniscient God—unlike both Gus and poor old Pat, "crunched" to death by Moore. (In a way, *Arcadia* itself demonstrates chaos theory. What really happened in the nineteenth century—just as what occurs at any point in history—is too complicated for any human being to figure out, including Jarvis. It's also too complicated for the playwright to fully represent.) Or at least, if not immortal, Lightning resembles one whose "chief power is precisely to hold in a simultaneous perception moments, events, men, and causes which are humanly dispersed through time" (Barthes, *Michelet,* 22).[35]

You will have observed an abundance of both death and sex here. (The play opens with Thomasina, age thirteen, asking: "Septimus, what is carnal embrace?" "Carnal embrace," Hodge hedges, "is the practice of throwing one's arms around a side of beef" [1].) You'll have observed an abundance of erotic love too, which, as in *Indian Ink,* does matter. But what matters most is the pursuit of knowledge, including self-knowledge, which Nightingale associates with literary enthusiasm.[36] "If knowledge isn't self-knowledge it isn't doing much, mate," he asserts sarcastically when Valentine dismisses the question "who wrote what when" as trivial in the scientific sense of the word, adding:

---

35. In *Arcadia*'s final scene, the play's two time periods do collapse into one another. The simultaneity in *The Invention of Love,* where a dying Housman encounters younger versions of himself, is not the same. That play, like *Travesties,* is under the old man's control.

36. See Fleming, 200–201: In its depiction of people striving to understand the past and to find the keys that unlock the mysteries of nature, *Arcadia* "is a celebration of the human struggle to obtain knowledge, with meaning arriving as much out of the process as the product." Stoppard, moreover, presents five characters engaged in the quest for knowledge: "Thomasina, Septimus, and Valentine are pursuing an understanding of the world from a scientific perspective, while Hannah and Bernard represent the arts and humanities. Characteristic of Stoppard's desire to complicate matters, the three 'scientists' are the least Newtonian" (Fleming, 201). And since Jarvis and Thomasina prove correct about both human and natural history, the play, Fleming argues, "is an affirmation that despite all the indeterminacy, people can use their intellect and intuition to gain knowledge" (201). Jarvis, however, doesn't feel that way. Despite her relative accuracy, the scholar claims to know "nothing" about "anything"—a conceivably Socratic pose (*Arcadia,* 95). But Jarvis is despondent at the time, and so the only irony involved in that declaration would have to be dramatic.

> Is the universe expanding? Is it contracting? Is it standing on one
> leg and singing "When Father Painted the Parlour"? Leave me
> out. I can expand my universe without you. "She walks in beauty,
> like the night of cloudless climes and starry skies, and all that's
> best of dark and bright meet in her aspect and her eyes." There
> you are, he wrote it after coming from a party. (*Arcadia,* 61)

It's a dismissal Jarvis rejects as well, but without sarcasm—or
egocentrism:

> It's *all* trivial—your grouse, my hermit, Bernard's Byron. Com-
> paring what we're looking for misses the point. It's wanting to
> know that makes us matter. Otherwise we're going out the way
> we came in. That's why you can't believe in the afterlife, Valen-
> tine. Believe in the after, by all means, but not the life. Believe
> in God, the soul, the spirit, the infinite, believe in angels if you
> like, but not the great celestial get-together for an exchange of
> views. If the answers are in the back of the book I can wait, but
> what a drag. Better to struggle on knowing that failure is final.
> (75–76, emphasis original)

It's also one Hodge rejects, with Socratic irony: "I do not rule,"
the hermit-to-be tells Augustus. "I inspire by reverence for learn-
ing and the exaltation of knowledge whereby man may approach
God" (80).

There's no tortoise in *The Invention of Love* (1997). Nor, for
Housman, is there carnal knowledge. The playwright seems to believe that scholars don't, or can't, have sex: first Moore, then Jarvis,
now Housman. Like my version of Proust, moreover, Stoppard's
version of the poet and scholar doesn't even touch anyone he desires. This is so, in part, because the only one he desired—an athletic classmate named Moses Jackson—wasn't gay. For Stoppard's
Wilde, however, there's carnal knowledge aplenty.[37] This is so
because the one he desired—Lord Alfred Douglas (or "Bosie")—
was. Even so, both poet and playwright (Wilde, that is) see love
the same way. Housman tells his younger self:

---

37. See Zeifman: The play shows both the romantic individualist (Wilde) celebrated
yet punished for his authenticity and the repressed classicist (Housman) refusing
the chaos of emotion.

In the Dark Ages, in Macedonia, in the last guttering light from classical antiquity, a man copied out bits from old books for his young son, whose name was Septimius [not Septimus]; so we have one sentence from *The Loves of Achilles*. Love, said Sophocles, is like the ice held in the hand by children. A piece of ice held fast in the fist. (*Invention of Love*, 43)

(This omits Sophocles' explanation that however much pleasure the ice gives to start with, the children end up being able neither to hold it nor to let it go. Love, moreover, was heat in both *Indian Ink* and *Arcadia*.) Wilde—more Stendhalian now than Foucauldian—tells Housman:

The betrayal of oneself is lifelong regret. Bosie is what became of me. He is spoiled, vindictive, utterly selfish, and not very talented, but these are merely the facts. The truth is he was Hyacinth when Apollo loved him, he is ivory and gold, from his red rose-leaf lips comes music that fills me with joy, he is the only one who understands me. "Even as a teething child throbs with ferment, so does the soul of him who gazes upon the boy's beauty; he can neither sleep at night nor keep still by day," and a lot more besides, but before Plato could describe love, the loved one had to be invented. We would never love anyone if we could see past our invention. Bosie is my creation, my poem. In the mirror of invention, love discovered itself. Then we saw what we had made—the piece of ice in the fist you cannot hold or let go. (95)[38]

The play does, however, contain a desk. We see Housman seated at a rather neat one, surrounded by books, inkpot, and pen, and recovering plenty of information about classical antiquity. For whereas Housman the poet, having almost never been to the county, probably used that desk to apostrophize Shropshire lads, Housman the scholar (or philologist) is using it "to establish what the ancient authors really wrote"—even in

---

38. See Fleming, 241: Sophocles' explanation "aptly summarizes both Housman's and Wilde's experiences with love: Housman could not hold on to Jackson, while Wilde could never let go of Lord Alfred Douglas."

the absence of autographs (24).[39] All he has are corrupt copies. Unlike Wilde, Housman is a closet case; yet the desk, for some reason, hasn't a secret compartment, nor even any drawers. The recovery job, moreover, involves straightening up other scholars' mess: "When I with some thought and some pains have got this rather uninteresting garden into decent order, here is Dr. Postgate hacking at the fence in a spirited attempt to reestablish chaos amongst Propertius manuscripts" (81). Housman considers academics like Postgate nothing but "literary critic[s] in dead languages" (47).

Housman also tells his younger self what knowledge is, or rather what it isn't. "Literary enthusiasm never made a scholar, and unmade many," he instructs. "Taste is not knowledge" (37). The lesson takes: "Scholarship is nothing to do with taste," we later hear the lad tell Alfred Pollard, another classmate (69). Wilde, of course, disagrees. Less scholarly than Housman, he instructs that knowledge—of truth, as opposed to mere fact (Bosie as "ivory and gold," not spoiled and vindictive)—involves imaginative misrepresentation. "A scholar is all scruple, an artist is none," Wilde tells Housman. "The artist must lie, cheat, deceive, be untrue to nature and contemptuous of history" (96).

What Housman does come to know is that life is meaningless. "You think there is an answer: the lost autograph copy of life's meaning, which we might recover from the corruptions that have made it nonsense," he also instructs. "But if there is no such copy, really and truly there is no answer" (41). (For Housman, then, any answers aren't so much in back of the book as in front.) Such knowledge is attributable, in part, to the man's atheism, or to his never having known God. Whereas Jarvis the scholar may not believe in an afterlife, at least she lets Valentine the scientist believe in God. Housman the scholar won't let Pollard: Given how much of the historical record has been destroyed, the only possible knowledge, he says, is partial. In other words, there's no

---

39. Stoppard, *Invention of Love*, 36: For the playwright's Housman, one can't be good at both endeavors because "poetical feelings are a peril to scholarship." The poetic playwright, however, proves a masterful scholar of both Housman and Wilde. He does so, moreover, despite a failure to have experienced any gay milieu firsthand—as far as I know.

such thing as omniscience for Housman, no such thing as a ceiling view. And although scholarship may be "where we're nearest to our humanness," it's all "useless knowledge for its own sake."

> Useful knowledge is good, too, but it's for the faint-hearted, an elaboration of the real thing, which is only to shine some light, it doesn't matter where on what, it's the light itself, against the darkness, it's what's left of God's purpose when you take away God. (71)[40]

Housman's knowledge is also attributable to his loneliness, or to his never having known the beloved.[41] For whereas Thomasina (the scientist) was ahead of her time, Housman (the lover) is behind: He and Jackson, he feels, should have been Achilles and Patroclus. Of course, what Housman doesn't seem to realize, as Stoppard does, is that heroic comradeship—long before Socrates—was asexual.

Stoppard's moral: Self-examination through literary enthusiasm—or linguistic mediation—doesn't always work. Nightingale the academic may know himself as Byron, to a certain extent: The two have things in common. Wilde the artist may know himself as Apollo. Nor need literary enthusiasm impede clearsighted acceptance of one's beloved creation as he really is, at his worst. Bosie, Wilde realizes, is both "ivory and gold" and spoiled. (Was Bosie ever at his best? Was there ever any more to him? I imagine not.) But just as Henry Carr is no Algernon Moncrieff and his wife no Cecily, Housman the scholar is no Achilles and Jackson no Patroclus. By imagining himself a heroic comrade, moreover, Housman fails to situate himself within history. (Wilde might say he's "contemptuous.") Like Carr, that is, he fails to recover the truth—or rather, to remember the facts—of his own distant past. For whereas Wilde ends *The Invention of Love* with the epigram "Nothing that actually occurs is of the smallest

---

40. See Fleming, 243: *The Invention of Love* concerns "the passionate, relentless search for truth and meaning as a defining feature of humanity even as access to ultimate meaning remains elusive."

41. Despite his accuracy, Housman claims to know relatively little about anything—another conceivably Socratic pose. But he's even more despondent than Jarvis, and so the only irony involved—including the irony of this repetition from play to play—is dramatic.

importance" (102), Housman, like Cecily, ends by indicating he's misconstrued his youth:

> Which is not to say I have remembered it right, messing about
> in a boat with Moses and dear old Pollard on a summer's day
> in '79 or '80 or '81; but not impossible, not so out of court
> as to count as an untruth in the dream-warp of the ultimate
> room, though the dog is still in question. And yet not dreaming
> either, wide awake to all the risks—archaism, anachronism, the
> wayward inconsequence that only hindsight can acquit of *non
> sequitur, quietus interruptus* by monologue incontinent in the
> hind leg of a donkey class (you're too kind but I'm not there yet),
> and the unities out of the window without so much as a win-
> dow to be out of: still shaky, too, from that first plummet into
> bathos, Greek for depth but in rhetoric a ludicrous descent from
> the elevated to the commonplace, as it might be from Virgil
> to Jerome K. Jerome if that is even a downward slope at time of
> speaking, and when is *that*?—for walking on water is not among
> my party tricks, the water and the walking work it out between
> them. Neither dead nor dreaming, then, but in between, not
> short on fact, or fiction, and suitably attired in leather boots, the
> very ones I was too clever for, which—here comes the fact—I left
> in my will to my college servant. (100–101, emphasis original)

The allusion, I'm certain, is to Jerome's *Three Men in a Boat (To Say Nothing of the Dog)*. I imagine it's also to *The Death of Virgil*, by Hermann Broch. And to Joyce. Housman's final monologue isn't really "incontinent," or logorrheic. It's stream-of-consciousness.

Or if you prefer, "Some Final Words" of Billy Collins (in *The Art of Drowning*):

> The past is nothing,
>> a nonmemory, a phantom,
>> a soundproof closet in which Johann Strauss
>> is composing another waltz no one can hear.

It's a "fabrication, best forgotten." So forget Strauss.

And forget his younger brother,
the poor bastard who was killed in a fall
from a podium while conducting a symphony.
Forget the past,
forget the stunned audience on its feet,
the absurdity of their formal clothes
in the face of sudden death,
forget their collective gasp,
the murmur and huddle over the body,
the creaking of the lowered curtain.

Forget Strauss
with that encore look in his eye
and his tiresome industry:
more than five hundred finished compositions!
He even wrote a polka for his mother.
That alone is enough to make me flee the past,
evacuate its temples,
and walk alone under the stars
down these dark paths strewn with acorns,
feeling nothing but the crisp October air,
the swing of my arms
and the rhythm of my stepping—
a man of the present who has forgotten
every composer, every great battle,
just me,
a thin reed blowing in the night. (82–83)

MOVABLE TYPE

Public postures have the configuration of private derangement.
—*Stoppard*, The Real Thing

Now that I know Bruce Chatwin's life nearly as well as his work, I must confess I don't like it a lot. Or rather, I don't like him. For one thing, Chatwin took advantage of friends. He also took advantage of his wife, Elizabeth Chanler. So I'm tempted to deprecate him—much as Chatwin treated Indira Gandhi, that "lying, scheming bitch" (quoted in Shakespeare, 298).[1] But I'm stopped by the Proustian recognition that an author's best, possibly truest self is in the work alone.[2] I'm stopped by the death of

---

1. For Chatwin's treatment, see "On the Road with Mrs. G." in *What Am I Doing Here,* 316–40.
2. See Nietzsche, 236–37 (emphasis original): "The ceaseless desire to create on the part of the artist, together with his ceaseless observation of the world outside him, prevent him from becoming better and more beautiful as a person, that is to say from creating *himself*—except, that is, if his self-respect is sufficiently great to compel him to exhibit himself before others as being as great and beautiful as his works increasingly are. In any event, he possesses only a fixed quantity of strength: that of it which he expends upon *himself*—how could he at the same time expend it on his *work*?—and the reverse."

the author—not so much in a figurative, Barthesian sense (why pick on someone who doesn't exist?) as in a literal one (why pick on someone who doesn't exist *anymore*?). Like James Boatwright and Robert Phelps, elegized by Howard, Chatwin died of AIDS at forty-eight. I'm also stopped by the recognition that we're a lot alike. Much as Chatwin found Robert Louis Stevenson disturbingly familiar (that egoist with a "morbid" concern for his public image, "girlish" attraction to aggressive men, and "bizarre" marriage to Fanny Osbourne ["The Road to the Isles," in *Anatomy of Restlessness,* 130, 136]), I find Chatwin so: Mr. Hyde to my Dr. Jekyll.[3]

And now that I know Chatwin's work habits as well as his work, I must confess I'm surprised by them. Given how well traveled and gregarious he was, I pictured him in truly public spaces—railway stations, hotel lobbies, coffee shops—which of course doesn't make sense for someone who deprecated urban settlement. I even pictured him there after I began "A Tower in Tuscany," which mentions private rooms. "Those of us who presume to write books would appear to fall into two categories," according to Chatwin's introduction: the ones who "dig in" and the ones who move:

> There are writers who can only function "at home," with
> the right chair, the shelves of dictionaries and encyclopedias,
> and now perhaps the word processor. And there are those,
> like myself, who are paralyzed by "home," for whom home is
> synonymous with the proverbial writer's block, and who believe
> naively that all would be well if only they were somewhere
> else. Even among the very great you find the same dichotomy:
> Flaubert and Tolstoy laboring in their libraries; Zola with a suit
> of armor alongside his desk; Poe in his cottage; Proust in the
> cork-lined room. On the other hand, among the "movers" you
> have Melville, who was "undone" by his gentlemanly establish-
> ment in Massachusetts, or Hemingway, Gogol, or Dostoyevsky,
> whose lives, whether from choice or necessity, were a headlong

---

3. See Clapp, 128: Chatwin's review of one Stevenson biography "is that of someone fighting off fascination and complicity." The review, moreover, is "a complicated piece of self-examination and self-dislike."

round of hotels and rented rooms—and, in the case of the last, a
Siberian prison. (*Anatomy*, 22)

After all, there are plenty of reasons such a person, more Baudelaire's flaneur than Benjamin's, would prefer such places: to avoid
loneliness; to experience community (despite anonymity); to
discover inspiration (overheard conversations, overseen incidents,
unforeseen encounters); to confirm identity ("If that man sees
me writing, I must be a writer"); to encourage address ("I'll write
to *him*"—not that writing in public guarantees address [think
of Benjamin], nor is it a requirement [think of Barthes cruising
readers in the privacy of his bedroom]); or to eroticize address, if
the man's attractive. (Many found Chatwin irresistible.) You can
also cruise there in the nonmetaphorical sense of the word, and
then it's back to the room for the two of you. The book can wait.
Chatwin, moreover, indicates what I misconstrued as a formative
stage of the protocol preference, not to mention the sexual orien-
tation. "My early childhood was war and the feeling of war," he
writes in an unpublished draft of *In Patagonia* (quoted in Clapp,
54). (The allusion is to Wilfred Owen: "My subject is war and
the pity of war.")

> We were homeless and adrift. My father was at sea, my mother
> and I wandering from place to place, traveling up and down
> wartime England to stay with relations and friends. Our tem-
> porary stopping-places are less clear than the journeys between
> them. The houses are unreal. I still have a horror of home. The
> real things are the slamming of train doors, the comfortable
> rumble of railway carriages, moquette-covered seats smelling
> of stale tobacco, canvas kitbags thrust through windows, or the
> white smile of a black G.I. across a half-lit station. (Chatwin,
> quoted in Clapp, 54–55)

The account omits the writer's younger brother Hugh, a familiar
paralipsis. (Proust omits brother Robert; Barthes, for that matter,
omits his brother in both the autobiography and *Camera Lucida*.)
"Horror of home" alludes to Baudelaire.

But Chatwin didn't write in railway stations, or at least didn't
write books there. He used those friends' homes, arranging rooms

to suit his needs and disarranging as work progressed.[4] (He also used fountain pens, legal pads, and finally typewriters.)[5] "Spent the morning clearing and organizing my study and the latter part of the afternoon fiddling with the book," notes one diary. "Less unhappy now than I was" (quoted in Shakespeare, 250). (He abandoned the diary shortly thereafter: *"Hate* confessional mode," notes one notebook [quoted in Shakespeare, 250, emphasis original].) "Whenever I have been in residence," concludes "A Tower in Tuscany," "the place becomes a sea of books and papers and unmade beds and clothes thrown this way and that" (in *Anatomy,* 26).

Chatwin appears indifferent to the kind of desk available: elevation alone mattered. (Diana Melly once found herself sawing at table legs he pronounced too long for composition.) A folding card table might do, despite the instability.[6] Or even a retractable shelf, despite the mobility. To quote "Bruce," the Proustian narrator of Chatwin's *Songlines,* as he describes arranging someone's trailer:

> There was a plyboard top which pulled out over the second bunk to make a desk. There was even a swiveling office chair. I put my pencils in a tumbler and my Swiss Army knife beside them. I unpacked some exercise pads and, with the obsessive neatness that goes with the beginning of a project, I made three neat stacks of my "Paris" notebooks. (160)[7]

Yet he's attracted to certain unusable desks, demonstrating an aesthetic interest in both Lenin's, with a bunch of asters on it, and Maxim Gorky's, with a bunch of knickknacks.[8] In his Welsh

---

4. According to Teddy Millington-Drake, Chatwin was "a remorseless shifter of desks and table lamps" (quoted in Clapp, 137). Unlike Barthes, however, he doesn't appear to have arranged them all the same way. Bishop, you recall, never wrote "anything of value at the desk where I was supposed to be doing it—it's always in someone else's house" (quoted in Millier, 544).

5. See Clapp, 204: Chatwin "graduated from Parker and Schaeffer pens to a Mont Blanc, liked to sharpen his pencils with a knife, not a pencil-sharpener, and produced his first drafts on . . . yellow legal pads." He then typed those drafts.

6. See Chatwin, "A Place to Hang Your Hat," in *Anatomy,* 18.

7. See Shakespeare, 442–43: "*The Songlines* is as much about nomads as it is about Bruce inventing himself as his best, most achieved character: intrepid and practical traveler, humble sage, sharp-witted inquisitor. This was Chatwin as he liked to see himself, a Hemingway hero full of deep feeling yet economical with words."

8. See Chatwin, "The Volga," in *What Am I,* 175.

novel, *On the Black Hill,* moreover, Benjamin and Lewis fetishize their dead mother's writing cabinet with its beautiful marquetry. Chatwin's also interested in a certain *ébéniste* from Dakar who specialized in "*bureaux-plats,* Louis Quinze and Louis Seize" (*Anatomy,* 53). (*Ébéniste* means "cabinetmaker"; *bureau-plat,* a flat-topped desk—the word is antiquarian.) "He was the best-looking boy I ever saw," Chatwin notes in a memoir not meant for publication (*Anatomy,* 52). The memoir's called "The Attractions of France," but may as well be called "When Sex Objects Make Art Objects and the Art Objects Are Desks."

Chatwin couldn't work in his own home because he was distracted by otherwise valued possessions and because he needed an audience other than Chanler.[9] (Other writers, you recall, abandon studies too organized, too disorganized, or simply too familiar to work in.) An indefatigable talker who rehearsed things before writing them down, Chatwin also recited work in progress both to himself, doing different voices, and to hosts to see if it held their interest.[10] (Salman Rushdie never met anyone who talked so much: "He was a magnificent raconteur of Scheherazadean inexhaustibility" ["Chatwin's Travels," 237]. Michael Krüger, Chatwin's German publisher, never met anyone who talked so quickly: "It was psychotic, not making an end, and, whenever interrupted, zigzagging back" [quoted in Shakespeare, 468].) The man was a magpie, and for more than one reason: "Chatty" Chatwin was a bit of a thief.[11] Other birds came to mind too. Teddy Millington-Drake considered Chatwin a cuckoo because he "made his nest in whatever part of the house he had been assigned [and then moved on to] someone else's" (quoted in McEwen, 122). Chatwin

---

9. Cf. Nietzsche, 159: "Socrates found the kind of wife he needed—but even he would not have sought her if he had known her well enough: the heroism of even this free spirit would not have extended to that. For Xantippe in fact propelled him deeper and deeper into his own proper profession, inasmuch as she made his house and home uncomfortable and unhomely to him: she taught him to live in the street and everywhere where one could chatter and be idle, and thus fashioned him into the greatest Athenian street-dialectician."

10. Some hosts never lost interest: "Bruce would get up and pace around and sometimes—damagingly, for he made everything seem equally entertaining—read bits aloud" (Clapp, 33).

11. See Shakespeare, 408: Loulou de la Falaise saw Chatwin as a *pique-assiette* (someone who eats off another's plate).

considered himself various migratory birds, having both "a compulsion to wander and a compulsion to return" ("Letter to Tom Maschler," in *Anatomy*, 76): a swallow at first and then an Arctic tern, the "beautiful white bird what flies from the North Pole to the South Pole and back again" (*Songlines*, 278).[12] But he also considered himself a bowerbird, arranging his home with bits of this and that to attract a mate—or simply to please himself.

Chatwin did have a dual personality and so, like Stoppard, was interested in (non)identical twins. (Think of Jacob and Esau.) For the playwright, "one has a public self and a submerged self," or rather, "a complex personality only part of which runs the show" (quoted in Gussow, 79, 80).[13] For the travel writer, one is both civilized and primitive, both careworn city dweller (or Cain) and carefree nomad (Abel).[14] In *On the Black Hill*, for example, Benjamin is Cain; Lewis his twin, Abel. (Benjamin and Lewis are really "Bruce and Bruce," according to Jonathan Hope: "He would have loved to have had an identical twin" [quoted in Shakespeare, 403].) But whereas Chatwin imagined Abel running the show, others noticed Cain. Murray Bail found that traveling with Chatwin in India was "like traveling with Garbo"—the amount of luggage was simply "colossal" (quoted in Shakespeare, 480). John Pawson found that a writer's retreat he designed for Chatwin

---

12. See *The Songlines*, 161: "Could it be," Chatwin asks, "that our need for distraction, our mania for the new, was, in essence, an instinctive migratory urge akin to that of birds in autumn?" See also Chatwin, "I Always Wanted to Go to Patagonia," in *Anatomy*, 6.

13. See Delaney, 26: "*The Invention of Love* shows us Housman as young and old, as poet and critic, as passionate lover and repressed celibate. *Hapgood* dramatizes the coolly professional buttoned-down title character and a woman who appears to be her raucous, impetuous twin in a play that uses quantum mechanics as a metaphor for the ineluctable duality of human personality. But Stoppard was also . . . the author of *Arcadia* in which romantic impetuosity and classical restraint are as interwoven in personal temperament as in poetry. Even *Rosencrantz and Guildenstern Are Dead* contains, in the contrast between its two title characters, a sense of the multiple possibilities of identity." *Hapgood* uses quantum mechanics by analogizing dual personality to the dual (wave/particle) nature of light.

14. Chatwin recognized other dualities as well. See, e.g., Chatwin, "Among the Ruins," in *Anatomy*, 152: "Given the tenuous borderline between extremes of asceticism and of sensuality, the 'good' Tiberius is probably the same as the 'bad.'" Barthes, of course, could envision a multitudinous self. See Smith, 108.

was far less Spartan than his client imagined.[15] ("I don't do much writing in my [Eaton Place apartment]," Chatwin confessed. "For that, I need other conditions and other places. But I can think there, listen to music, read in bed, and take notes" ["A Place to Hang Your Hat," in *Anatomy*, 21].) And then there's everything Chatwin left for Chanler to manage. According to Gillian Walker, the husband "could have the illusion of nomadic existence" only because the wife maintained his vast collections (quoted in Shakespeare, 570). According to Pattie Sullivan, he could do so only "because Elizabeth sat in the country with a warehouse of the stuff he'd acquired" (quoted in Shakespeare, 269). (Recall Proust's dependence on Céleste Albaret or Ingres's on Madeleine Chapelle.) Walker and Sullivan are, of course, accusing Chatwin of pretense, much as I accused Barthes. Or maybe of disavowal: a dual consciousness, as with fantasy or hallucination. Or maybe bad faith in Sartre's sense: The man doesn't even know he's kidding himself. (A unitary consciousness, as with false consciousness or ideological subjection.) Then again, whom are *we* kidding?

"Nomadic," however, is the wrong word for the unsettled side of Chatwin's personality. So is "migratory." True nomads don't move about in readerly ways: seeking sensation and/or adventure, self-discovery and/or self-extinction.[16] They aren't trying to escape anything. Nor do nomads move randomly. They move through the same places repeatedly, cyclically—seeking pasture.[17] They both know and understand these places, moreover, and so have a strong sense of them as home. Plus they're illiterate, even according to Chatwin.[18] Whereas there is, of course, nomadic speech, or storytelling, there's no such thing as nomadic writing—an aporia the writer himself recognized. His unfinished, unfinishable book on nomads, Chatwin says, even contained a "diatribe" against the act of writing ("I Always Wanted to Go to Patagonia," in *Anatomy*,

---

15. See Shakespeare, 467.
16. In Chatwin's *Viceroy of Ouidah*, Francisco wanders off "in search of a self that continually eludes him" (Meanor, 51).
17. See Chatwin, "Abel the Nomad," in *Anatomy*, 113: "A nomad proper is a herdsman who moves his property through a sequence of pastures."
18. See, e.g., Chatwin, "Letter to Tom Maschler," in *Anatomy*, 78.

13).[19] He also has *The Songlines'* Bruce claim to have realized the absurdity of such a book after reading a certain text from the Chinese *Book of Odes:*

> Useless to ask a wandering man
> Advice on the construction of a house.
> The work will never come to completion. (*Songlines,* 178)

In fact, the only reason Chatwin should be seen as either nomadic or migratory, according to biographer Nicholas Shakespeare, is that his twin poles "consisted of the road and the writing desk" (249).

(According to Adorno, "prosperous Puritans vainly try to get from the dark-haired denizens of foreign countries what the course of the world, which they control, denies not only to them but all the more to the vagrants. The sedentary man envies the nomadic existence, the quest for fresh pastures, and the painted wagon is the house on wheels whose course follows the stars. Infantility, fixated in desultory motion, the joylessly restless, momentary urge to survive, stands in for the undistorted, for fulfillment, and yet excludes it, inwardly resembling the self-preservation from which it falsely promises deliverance. This is the circle of bourgeois nostalgia for naivete" [170].)

So what's the right word? (According to Barthes, of course, stereotypes are untruthful—except for ones like Flying Dutchman.) Apart from seeing himself as a nomad, and more importantly apart from seeing himself as either a settler or collector, Chatwin tried "gypsy." He tried both "vagabond" and "literary vagabond"—after role model Rimbaud but also after Walt Whitman and Hart Crane, all poets, of course. Not after Stevenson. He tried both "wanderer" and "Wandering Jew." ("No people but the Jews have ever felt more keenly the moral ambiguities of settlement" [Chatwin, *Songlines,* 194].) Best of all, he tried

---

19. The book was to have argued "that in becoming human, man had acquired, together with his straight legs and striding walk, a migratory 'drive' or instinct to walk long distances through the seasons; that this 'drive' was inseparable from his central nervous system; and that, when warped in conditions of settlement, it found outlets in violence, greed, status-seeking, or a mania for the new" ("I Always Wanted to Go to Patagonia," in *Anatomy,* 12).

"traveler."[20] (Not "flaneur," not "tourist," never "sexual tourist.")[21] Travelers really work, for Chatwin. "The word travel is the same as the French *travail*," he told Michael Ignatieff.

CHATWIN: It means hard work, penance, and finally a journey. There was an idea, particularly in the Middle Ages, that by going on a pilgrimage, as Muslim pilgrims do, you were reinstating the original condition of man. The act of walking through a wilderness was thought to bring you back to God. That is something you find in all the religions.

IGNATIEFF: Do you think of your traveling in terms of pilgrimage?

CHATWIN: Pilgrimage is too strong, really. It's just that I'm a footloose sort of character and can't do anything else.

IGNATIEFF: Do you think of yourself as a travel writer?

CHATWIN: It always irritated me to be called a travel writer. So I decided to write something about people who never went out. That's how *On the Black Hill* came into being.

IGNATIEFF: But it is true that you yourself can't write unless you travel.

CHATWIN: That's very true.

IGNATIEFF: Then the question is why?

CHATWIN: I wish I knew. I do find it quite interesting that in one form or another all the great early epics—whether it's the *Odyssey* or *Beowulf*—are traveler's tales. Why should it be that the metaphor of the voyage is at the heart of all story-telling? It's not simply that most stories are traveler's tales, it's actually the way these epics are patterned into a voyage structure. (Ignatieff, 27–28)

---

20. See "I Always Wanted to Go to Patagonia," in *Anatomy*, 12 (gypsy), 134 (vagabond, literary vagabond), 190 (wanderer, Wandering Jew). See also Shakespeare, 45: "I have never felt any real attachment to a home and fail to produce the normal emotive response when the word is mentioned," Chatwin tells himself in one notebook, "except when traveling."

21. See Chatwin, "The Nomadic Alternative," in *Anatomy*, 85: "It is an emotional rather than a rational impulse that has always led men to abandon civilization and seek a simpler life, a life in harmony with 'nature,' unhampered with possessions, free from the grinding bonds of technology, sinless, promiscuous, anarchic, and sometimes vegetarian."

Another advantage of the traveler stereotype is that it connotes the creation of order out of chaos. Baudelaire, in *"Invitation au voyage,"* wrote, *"Là, tout n'est q'ordre et beauté, / Luxe, calme et volupté"* (58) ("There, everything is order and beauty, / Luxury, calm, and pleasure"). It's a line Chatwin loved.

Although he never called himself a travel writer, Chatwin did call himself a storyteller. (Not, however, an Ancient Mariner—perhaps too old a figure for Chatwin, who, if so, doesn't realize that the Wandering Jew is even older.)[22] "I've always loved telling stories," he told Colin Thubron. "Everyone says, 'Are you writing a novel?' No, I'm writing a story and I do insist that things must be called stories. That seems to me to be what they are. I don't quite know the meaning of the word novel" (quoted in Shakespeare, 11). (Recall Barthes's claiming not to know what an "influence" is.) The figure comports with Chatwin's logorrhea as well as with his "footloose" character: hence his identification with Homer and Dante—both poets, once again. (Chatwin, quoting Mandelstam on Dante: "The question occurs to me—and quite seriously—how many shoe soles, how many ox-hide soles, how many sandals Alighieri wore out in the course of his poetic work, wandering about on the goat paths of Italy" [*Songlines,* 229]. Mandelstam, according to Chatwin, "could *only* compose on the hoof" [quoted in Ignatieff, 37, emphasis original]. Chatwin himself did prefer traveling on foot, or "walking through a wilderness.") In other words, Chatwin (literally) moved about in writerly ways too: both walking and, well, not talking; both walking and, well, not quite working but playing with language and form—as if writing poetry.[23] (I say this regardless of that line about travel and

22. See Chatwin, *In Patagonia,* 90: Coleridge was "'a night-wandering man,' a stranger at his own birthplace, a drifter round rooming-houses, unable to sink roots anywhere. He had a bad case of what Baudelaire called 'The Great Malady: Horror of One's Home.' Hence his identification with other blighted wanderers: Cain, the Wandering Jew, or the horizon-struck navigators of the sixteenth century. For the Mariner was himself." And 130: "Poe, like Coleridge whom he idolized, was another night-wandering man, obsessed by the Far South and by voyages of annihilation and rebirth—an enthusiasm he would pass on to Baudelaire." Chatwin appreciates chains of literary identification even if they don't seem to include him.
23. See Shakespeare, 325, quoting Clapp on Chatwin's style: "A teasing hovering between fact and fiction; a combination of a very spare syntax and short simple sentences, with a rich flamboyant vocabulary, lots of arcane words, lots of peculiarities,

travail: intellectual labor isn't the same as physical.)[24] The figure also comports with his nomad fantasy. Hence his identification with native Australians, and of his "stories" with their "dreaming-tracks" or "songlines." Of course, much of Chatwin is far more Proustian than aboriginal. He assimilates "elements of reportage, autobiography, ethnology, the Continental tradition of the essay, and even gossip," to quote Hans Magnus Enzensberger (657). And of course, now that Chatwin's dead, the story of his own life—the biography—seems far more novelistic than the writer himself could have known at the time. If, that is, you believe Benjamin on both open-ended stories and death-driven novels:

> A man listening to a story is in the company of the story-teller; even a man reading one shares this companionship. The reader of a novel, however, is isolated, more so than any other reader. (For even the reader of a poem is ready to utter the words, for the benefit of the listener.) In this solitude of his, the reader of a novel seizes upon his material more jealously than anyone else. He is ready to make it completely his own, to devour it, as it were. Indeed, he destroys, he swallows up the material as the fire devours logs in the fireplace. The suspense which permeates the novel is very much like the draft which stimulates the flame in the fireplace and enlivens its play.
>
> It is a dry material on which the burning interest of the reader feeds. "A man who dies at the age of thirty-five," said Moritz Heimann once, "is at every point of his life a man who dies at the age of thirty-five." Nothing is more dubious than this sentence—but for the sole reason that the tense is wrong. A man—so says the truth that was meant here—who died at thirty-five will appear to *remembrance* at every point in his life as a man who dies at the age of thirty-five. In other words, the statement that makes no sense for real life becomes indisputable

---

and a non-chronological, rather elliptical structure." Chatwin would call his style nomadic: "portable, asymmetric, discordant, restless, incorporeal, and intuitive" ("The Nomadic Alternative," in *Anatomy,* 98).

24. See "Abel the Nomad," in *Anatomy,* 113: "Mr. [Wilfred] Thesiger is not a nomad but a traveler, in whom the old sense of travel as 'travail' has been revived: at one point he writes that the cartilages in his knee wore out and he had to have them removed."

for remembered life. The nature of the character in a novel cannot be presented any better than is done in this statement, which says that the "meaning" of his life is revealed only in his death. But the reader of a novel actually does look for human beings from whom he derives the "meaning of life." Therefore he must, no matter what, know in advance that he will share their experience of death: if need be their figurative death—the end of the novel—but preferably their actual one. How do the characters make him understand that death is already waiting for them—a very definite death and at a very definite place? That is the question which feeds the reader's consuming interest in the events of the novel.

The novel is significant, therefore, not because it presents someone else's fate to us, perhaps didactically, but because this stranger's fate by virtue of the flame which consumes it yields us the warmth which we never draw from our own fate. What draws the reader to the novel is the hope of warming his shivering life with a death he reads about. ("The Storyteller" 100–101, emphasis original)[25]

Yet for Enzenberger, to continue that quotation, "there is a haunting presence, something . . . solitary" (657), underneath the brilliance of Chatwin's storytelling. And Chatwin was solitary, according to one who knew him well. "He was dead lonely and he took it with him into the desert," says Howard Hodgkin. "It was the one thing Elizabeth couldn't do anything about" (quoted in Shakespeare, 402).

(Have I mentioned that Benjamin had a younger brother who committed suicide? Otherwise like Walter, Georg was the more ardent Communist—someone who secretly translated articles from *Pravda* into German despite the risks involved. The Gestapo did trace one such translation, for which he was sent to jail for six years and then to a concentration camp. It was there that Georg killed himself. According to an unaccountably omniscient biographer, "his thoughts were with [Walter] right up to the end" [Brodersen, 209].)

---

25. Stories, moreover, are "diegetic" in Plato's sense, "extradiegetic" in Genette's; novels are mimetic and intradiegetic.

Where Chatwin truly worked on writing was at the desk, not on the road. (I'll get to where he truly played.) "Fiddling" is the wrong word for this activity. ("Spent . . . the latter part of the afternoon fiddling with the book.") So is "stringing sentences together" the wrong description. (Chatwin, typically glib, said of *In Patagonia*: "While stringing its sentences together, I thought that telling stories was the only conceivable occupation for a superfluous person such as myself" ["I Always Wanted to Go to Patagonia," in *Anatomy*, 14]. Less glib, he once told a reporter that writing is like trying to make a single picture out of several different jigsaw puzzles.) I'd prefer the description "grinding away at sentences," to quote Barthes on Flaubert (*Writing Degree Zero*, 63), because Chatwin labored in his library as well—or someone else's. He struggled "to perfect his prose with . . . Flaubertian integrity," according to Francis Wyndham; artless spontaneity "was among the qualities that he least desired the result to express" (13).[26] (The same witness finds himself "acutely conscious of authorial *control*" when reading Chatwin, "and therefore, simultaneously and intoxicatingly, of the alluring danger of *loss* of control, of things getting out of hand" [quoted in Clapp, 42, emphasis original].) "How's the writing?" asks Arkady in *The Songlines*. "The usual mess," Bruce replies (284). (Arkady may represent a man named Toly Sawenko but, like Bruce, he also represents the author. Chatwin and Stoppard are twin dialecticians.)[27]

Critics refine Chatwin's self-characterizations. They suggest new ones as well. Instead of gypsy, for example, Rushdie calls Chatwin a scholar-gypsy; instead of storyteller, raconteur.[28] Rushdie also calls him a performer, thinking perhaps of Chatwin's frustrated acting career. Chanler concurs: "He was always playing a kind of role;

---

26. "Ow!" Chatwin wrote to Wyndham, "the strains of composition and of keeping up the momentum" (quoted in Shakespeare, 384). "Naturally his impulse was towards the baroque of his conversation and storytelling," writes Shakespeare. "He had to labor for his simplicity, discarding the ornate by first verbally sculpting the story, word by word, version after version, often, as he admitted, to the 'intense irritation' of his audience" (468).

27. See Rushdie, "Traveling with Chatwin," 233.

28. Rushdie, "Chatwin's Travels," 237: "He was a magnificent raconteur of Scheherazadean inexhaustibility, a gilt-edged name-dropper, a voracious reader of esoteric texts, a scholar-gypsy, a mimic—his Mrs. Gandhi was perfect—and a giggler of international class."

you could see him cooking up how he was going to do it" (quoted in Shakespeare, 10).[29] Patrick Meanor sees him as a combination action-hero/intellectual-hero, or *l'homme de bibliothèque*—like Malraux, one of the few writers Chatwin emulated who weren't poets.[30] Chatwin himself applauds Malraux's "happy mixture of intelligence and physical courage" but finds his otherwise "glorious" rhetoric unacceptable in English ("André Malraux," in *What Am I*, 133, 119). My favorite such characterization, though, is Roberto Calasso's:

> What tales of subterfuge, intrigue, conquest, and desolation emerge from the writings of the great scholars of central Asia . . . This is the ultimate exoticism: to read Markwart! To read Pelliot! To read Barthold! . . . Perhaps while leafing through the intoxicating pages of these philologists, Chatwin came across the word that, thinking about it now, describes him most accurately: *qalandar*. W. Ivanow once confessed that he spent forty years trying to define the term. To no avail. And the most that Henry Corbin would do was explain that in Persian poetry, the word, of pre-Islamic origin, was synonymous with "religious migrant, as free as the wind." Someone else defined these people as "wandering Dervishes, tellers of intricate tales, sons of kings often born in small apartments, sometimes crippled by fate." Very little is known about them for sure. But the sources always insist on two points: the real *qalandars* belong to no recognized religious cult and never sleep in the same place two nights running. (13–14, ellipses original)

Permit some characterizations of my own, despite a waning desire to know this at least former beloved. In addition to collector, I'd call Chatwin a *bibeloteur*—albeit one who can imagine the joy of voluntary dispossession.[31] "And do we not all long to throw

---

29. Clapp, 65: Chatwin was a "notable schoolboy actor" whose parents wouldn't let him make a career of it.

30. The list includes Proust and Hemingway, but Chatwin saw his own "bleak, chiseled style" as more like Hemingway's than Proust's ("My Modi," in *What Am I*, 366). Clapp comments: "He got as much pleasure from ejecting an adjective from his manuscript as he did from expelling an ornament from his flat" (31).

31. "The true collector houses a corps of inanimate lovers to shore up the wreckage of life," Chatwin writes. "The art collection, then, is a desperate stratagem against a

down our altars and rid ourselves of our possessions?" Chatwin asks rhetorically. "Do we not gaze coldly at our clutter and say, 'If these objects express my personality, then I hate my personality'" ("The Morality of Things," in *Anatomy,* 170).[32] His Czech novel, *Utz,* moreover, is about realizing that desire: helped by Marta, Utz liberates the two of them by destroying a priceless porcelain collection.[33] And in addition to the characterization cruiser, I would suggest "sexual tourist." (I've already had Chatwin "making and hallucinating connections wherever and whenever he happened to want sex or to address the reader," in "Same Place Twice.") There was that *ébéniste* from Dakar. There was also, to continue quoting from the few notebook entries that have been published, some "young Peul" in Mauritania: "The flatness of the face, the incredible sensitivity of the lips—the smile—the linear angularity of the mouth, the body sculptured, lithe, and vigorous" (King and Wyndham, 50).[34] (And God knows what we'll find when the notebooks—private documents never meant for publication—are open to inspection; they're at the Bodleian now and won't be available until 2010. Wyndham says they're simply "an accumulation of spontaneous jottings which try to pinpoint each incompletely realized reflection as it occurs in the tentative hope that it might one day be honed into a printable paragraph or

failure, a personal ritual to cure loneliness" ("The Morality of Things," in *Anatomy,* 172). I discuss Proust's bibelot renunciation in "Bedtime Story."

32. See Nietzsche, 284: "It is only up to a certain point that possessions make men more independent and free; one step further—and the possessions become master, the possessor becomes a slave: as which he must sacrifice to them his time and his thoughts and henceforth feel himself obligated to a society, nailed to a place, and incorporated into a state, none of which perhaps meets his inner and essential needs."

33. The novel is remarkably self-critical. See Clapp, 224: "Utz and his collection of porcelain are surrounded by present and historical variations on their theme: Utz's friend Dr. Orlik who collects flies; the Emperor Rudolf, who—among other exotica—collected the nails from Noah's Ark; Frederick William of Prussia, who collected giants; Bruce Chatwin, who collected collectors." It also indicates the author's loneliness. See Meanor, 145: Utz discovers how overwhelming the effort to maintain his collection had become only after finding "the ideal of true love, one he never knew he was looking for."

34. Cf. Barthes, "Incidents," 23: "Abdellatif—a voluptuous boy—peremptorily justifies the Baghdad hangings. The guilt of the accused is obvious, since the trial went so fast: the case was clear. Contradiction between the brutality of this nonsense and the fresh warmth of his body, the availability of his hands, which I continue, somewhat dazed, to hold and to caress while he pours out his vengeful catechism."

sentence and as a useful insurance against future amnesia" [12].
Redmond O'Hanlon says they're like "Gide with all the bits put
in" [quoted in Clapp, 204].) There was also some Patagonian pianist, a "nervous boy" who played for Chatwin and then probably
found him irresistible:

> He played the mazurka that Chopin dictated on his deathbed.
> The wind whistled in the street and the music ghosted from the
> piano as leaves over a headstone and you could imagine you were
> in the presence of genius. (*In Patagonia*, 25–26)

Chatwin calls the boy Anselmo, but his name was Enrique.[35]

And Steve? How would I characterize my brother? It's hard for
me to do so because I never knew him very well. But I've already
used "wanderer." ("Steve, that second Seymour who wandered off
to Israel over twenty years ago and then killed himself.") I'd say
"Zionist" as well, to clarify. And if not "genius," "intellectual."

Some people are good anywhere. "I don't much care where I
work," writes Annie Dillard. "I don't notice things" (42). Chatwin, however, always sought the ideal spot—almost "always becoming disillusioned or alighting on somewhere more desirable"
(Clapp, 150).[36] He claims to have found it twice. There was a
sixteenth-century home in India where staff waited on him hand
and foot. "A cool blue study overlooking the garden," he told Sunil
Sethi. "Bedroom giving out to the terrace. Unbelievably beautiful
girls who come with hot water, with real coffee, with papayas,
with a mango milkshake" (quoted in Shakespeare, 482). And
there was that tower in Tuscany—"built in the days of Guelph

---

35. See Shakespeare, 308: "Bruce told at least two people that he seduced Enrique,
although his notebook makes no reference to this."
36. Chatwin told one correspondent that he was always in search of "this mythi-
cal beast 'the place to write in'" (quoted in Shakespeare, 378). He even considered
owning one of his own. "He was ever looking to buy himself a bolt-hole in the
Vaucluse or Spain (in 1976, for instance, finding a 'little dream-house' in Alhaurin-
el-Grande: 'I think we'd better buy it,' he wrote to Gerald Brenan). Smallness was
a pre-requisite. 'Every time I saw in the countryside a one-room house with a window,' says [David] Sulzberger, 'I thought: "That's a Bruce Chatwin house."' While
walking with Loulou de la Falaise on the edge of Fontainebleau, Bruce spotted a
tool shed. 'This is the *perfect* place for writing in!' In 1986, on the brink of buying
land 'somewhere in the Mediterranean,' he outlined his ideal house to Pawson: 'I
need a courtyard, a flat roof with walls like a room open to the sky, 2 bedrooms
(1 a library-cum-bedroom), and a living-room-cum-kitchen with an open fire'"
(Shakespeare, 388, emphasis original).

and Ghibelline and standing on a hillside of oak and chestnut woods"—where it seems views didn't really matter. It had "very small windows that prevent you from getting distracted" (*Anatomy*, 23). (So you needn't note the elevation.) "Appealing workplaces are to be avoided," writes Dillard. "One wants a room with no view, so imagination can meet memory in the dark" (26).

They both sound nice. But to fully understand what Chatwin liked so much about them, let's revisit Eaton Place. Or rather, "A Place to Hang Your Hat," Chatwin's essay on the apartment. Here we find a formative stage of his true protocol preference. "Sometime in 1944, my mother and I went by train to see my father aboard his ship, the *Cynthia,* a U.S. minesweeper which had been lent to the British and had docked in Cardiff Harbor for a refit," the piece begins. "He was the captain. I was four years old."

> Once aboard, I stood in the crow's nest, yelled down the intercom, inspected the engines, ate plum pie in the ward-room; but the place I liked best was my father's cabin—a calm, functional space painted a calm pale gray; the bunk was covered in black oilcloth and, on a shelf, there was a picture of me.
>
> Afterwards, when he went back to sea, I liked to picture my father in the calm gray cabin, gazing at the waves from under the black-patent peak of his cap. And ever since, the rooms which have really appealed to my imagination have been ships' cabins, log cabins, monks' cells, or—although I have never been to Japan—the tea-house. (*Anatomy,* 15)

It is this space, this nest perhaps, that Chatwin had Pawson reconstruct: "I told him I wanted a cross between a cell and a ship's cabin" (*Anatomy,* 18).[37] (In other words, a movable cell—or shallop.) It is this space that accounts for Chatwin's obsessive neatness when arranging workrooms: Like his Dad, and like Proust, he preferred things shipshape. It may even account for the disarrangement description: a *sea* of books and papers. Dad's bed, of course,

---

37. The cell component of Chatwin's instruction may reflect an early childhood "hut dream." See *In Patagonia,* 3: "I pictured a low timber house with a shingled roof, caulked against storms, with blazing log fires inside and the walls lined with the best books, somewhere to live when the rest of the world blew up." And see Ignatieff, 36: "It is, of course, a fantasy of people like myself to sit in a cell and never move again." Compare Bishop's dream, which involved finding somewhere not to write.

corresponds to Chatwin's tidy desks—Argonautic replacements Barthes might appreciate. (The analogy, or homology: Bunk is to cabin as desk is to study.) But it doesn't correspond to them alone. It also corresponds to the neat little "Paris" notebooks, which Chatwin filled just about everywhere other than workrooms—the road, the railway station, you name it—and which are where he truly played with language, form, and information. Both the rectangular bed and the rectangular notebooks, he says, are covered in black oilcloth: "In France, these notebooks are known as *carnets moleskines: 'moleskine,'* in this case, being its black oilcloth binding" (*Songlines,* 160). Chatwin never makes the superficial connection. Nor does he detect the profound confusion. *Moleskine* is imitation leather, not oilcloth.

Both the untidy desks and the notebooks—their messy contents, rather—also correspond to one another: Like the interminable chatter, but not the writing, they both represent Chatwin's chaotic brain.[38] (Krüger: "It was psychotic, not making an end, and, whenever interrupted, zigzagging back.") That brain, in turn, represents, if not another cabin, a cabinet. "In my grandmother's dining-room there was a glass-fronted cabinet and in the cabinet a piece of skin," begins Chatwin's first book. "It was a small piece only, but thick and leathery, with strands of coarse, reddish hair. It was stuck to a card with a rusty pin. On the card was some writing in faded black ink, but I was too young then to read." But he wasn't too young for another protocol-related formative stage:

> "What's that?"
>
> "A piece of brontosaurus."
>
> My mother knew the names of two prehistoric animals, the brontosaurus and the mammoth. She knew it was not a mammoth. Mammoths came from Siberia.
>
> The brontosaurus, I learned, was an animal that had drowned in the Flood, being too big for Noah to ship aboard the Ark. I pictured a shaggy lumbering creature with claws and fangs and a malicious green light in its eyes. Sometimes the brontosaurus would crash through the bedroom wall and wake me from my sleep.

---

38. Cf. Gladwell, 93, once again: "The messy desk is not necessarily a sign of disorganization. It may be a sign of complexity: those who deal with many unresolved ideas simultaneously cannot sort and file the papers on their desks, because they haven't yet sorted and filed the ideas in their head."

This particular brontosaurus had lived in Patagonia, a country in South America, at the far end of the world. Thousands of years before, it had fallen into a glacier, traveled down a mountain in a prison of blue ice, and arrived in perfect condition at the bottom. Here my grandmother's cousin, Charley Milward the Sailor, found it. (*In Patagonia,* 1)

In reality, Charles Milward was one of the few travel writers Chatwin deliberately emulated.[39] That list includes Robert Byron and T. E. Lawrence. Milward's brontosaurus was really a giant sloth. And the cabinet contained more than just sloth skin. Rather full of curiosities, it was an old-fashioned *Wunderkammer,* according to art historian Robert Hughes.[40] A *Schatzkammer,* according to Hugh Honour. Honour calls Chatwin's own collection a *Schatzkammer* as well—one that, given the traveling, "mostly remained in his head." He calls the mind itself "an extraordinary jumble of the abstruse, the exotic, the savage, and the sophisticated," a *Schatzkammer* "filled to bursting with a miscellany of impressions which flowed out impetuously in his conversation" (quoted in Shakespeare, 8, 466).[41]

---

39. See *In Patagonia,* 148: Milward would "sit at a desk stirring his memory to recapture the ecstasy of going down to the sea in ships." And 149 (emphasis original): "Some of [his] yarns are a bit disordered and repetitive [but] *I* think they are wonderful." And 157: noting Milward's scrapbook entry about how whereas woman "stores her possessions about her, abiding with them," man "rides away, a tent dweller, an Arab with a horse and the plains about him." Milward, however, had no concern for his public image. And elevation mattered in a tower of his own.
40. See Shakespeare, 37.
41. See ibid.: "For Bruce, the lockable cabinet in West Heath Road was a sustaining metaphor [that] informed both the content of his work (faraway places, one-offs, marvels, fakes, the Beast) and its style (patchwork, vitreous, self-contained). The shelves and drawers were a repository for collecting, movement, and story. Bruce's life would enact all three. 'For those who are awake, the cosmos is one,' he wrote in his notebook, quoting Heraclitus. He hated to see a collection broken up." See also Meanor, 137: "Chatwin inevitably arrives at the creation of a mythopoeic world in all of his books: Mama Wéwé's syncretic menagerie in *[The Viceroy of Ouidah],* the native museums of the Salesian fathers in *In Patagonia,* the aboriginals' portable mythopoeic *tjuringas* in *The Songlines,* and [the painting] *The Broad and Narrow Path* in *On the Black Hill.* All of the novels' main characters require a private enshrinement of their sense of the sacred to sustain them in their wasteland world and give that world a spiritual dimension and meaning it would not otherwise have. In short, their private shrines transform the fallen world around them and restore it to its previous Edenic innocence. Utz's 'cabinet of curiosities' is his private shrine." Chatwin hung *The Broad and Narrow Path* above his own desk while writing *On the Black Hill.*

Have I mentioned Adorno on revision? "In his text," writes this refugee, "the writer sets up house."

> Just as he trundles papers, books, pencils, documents untidily
> from room to room, he creates the same disorder in his thoughts.
> They become pieces of furniture that he sinks into, content or
> irritable. He strokes them affectionately, wears them out, mixes
> them up, rearranges, ruins them. For a man who no longer has
> a homeland, writing becomes a place to live. In it he inevitably
> produces, as his family once did, refuse and lumber. But now
> he lacks a storeroom, and it is hard in any case to part from
> leftovers. So he pushes them along in front of him, in danger
> finally of filling his pages with them. The demand that one
> harden oneself against self-pity implies the technical necessity
> to counter any slackening of intellectual tension with the utmost
> alertness and to eliminate anything that has begun to encrust
> the work or to drift along idly, which may at an earlier stage
> have served, as gossip, to generate the warm atmosphere condu-
> cive to growth but is now left behind, flat and stale.

"In the end," he concludes, "the writer is not even allowed to live in his writing" (87).

Barthes found his *Schatzkammer* closer to the end of life. For reasons Chatwin himself should appreciate, this traveler (or sexual tourist) called Japan itself "The Cabinet of Signs": "In any and every site of this country, there occurs a special organization of space," concludes *Empire of Signs*.

> Traveling (in the street, in trains through the suburbs, over
> the mountains), I perceive the conjunction of a distance and
> a division, the juxtaposition of fields (in the rural and visual
> sense) simultaneously discontinuous and open (patches of tea
> plantations, of pines, of mauve flowers, a composition of black
> roofs, a grillwork of alleyways, a dissymmetrical arrangement
> of low houses): no enclosure (except for very low ones) and yet
> I am never besieged by the horizon (and its whiff of dreams):
> no craving to swell the lungs, to puff up the chest to make sure
> of my ego, to constitute myself as the assimilating center of
> the infinite: brought to the evidence of an empty limit, I am

limitless without the notion of grandeur, without a metaphysical reference.

It gets even more Proustian:

> From the slope of the mountains to the neighborhood inter-
> section, here everything is habitat, and I am always in the most
> luxurious room of this habitat: this luxury (which is elsewhere
> that of the kiosks, of corridors, of fanciful structures, collectors'
> cabinets, of private libraries) is created by the fact that the place
> has no other limit than its carpet of living sensations, of brilliant
> signs (flowers, windows, foliage, pictures, books); it is no longer
> the great continuous wall which defines space, but the very ab-
> straction of the fragments of view (of the "views") which frame
> me; the wall is destroyed beneath the inscription; the garden
> is a mineral tapestry of tiny volumes (stones, traces of the rake
> on the sand), the public place is a series of instantaneous events
> which accede to the notable in a flash so vivid, so tenuous that
> the sign does away with itself before any particular signified has
> had the time to "take." One might say that an age-old technique
> permits the landscape or the spectacle to produce itself, to occur
> in a pure significance, abrupt, empty, like a fracture. Empire of
> Signs? Yes, if it is understood that these signs are empty and that
> the ritual is without a god. Look at the cabinet of Signs (which
> was the Mallarmean habitat), i.e., in that country, any view,
> urban, domestic, rural, and the better to see how it is made,
> take for example the Shikidai gallery: tapestried with openings,
> framed with emptiness and framing nothing, decorated no
> doubt, but so that the figuration (flowers, trees, birds, animals)
> is removed, sublimated, displaced far from the foreground of the
> view, there is in it [no] place for furniture (a paradoxical word in
> French—*meuble*—since it generally designates a property any-
> thing but mobile, concerning which one does everything so that
> it will endure: with us, furniture has an immobilizing vocation,
> whereas in Japan the house, often deconstructed, is scarcely
> more than a furnishing—mobile—element); in the Shikidai
> gallery, as in the ideal Japanese house, stripped of furniture (or
> scantily furnished), there is no site which designates the slightest
> propriety in the strict sense of the word—ownership: neither

seat nor bed nor table out of which the body might constitute
itself as the subject (or master) of a space. (107–10)

You get the drift.

One reason Chatwin should appreciate the predication is that
teahouses appealed to his imagination "although I have never
been to Japan." Another is that, like Stoppard, he saw good writing as neither self-expressive nor original. ("No craving to swell
the lungs, to puff up the chest to make sure of my ego, to constitute myself as the assimilating center of the infinite.") "I'm unimpressed by the idea of the new," Chatwin told Ignatieff. "Most
advances in literature usually strike me as being advances into a
cul-de-sac" (Ignatieff, 28). (Bruce, upon hearing Arkady in a coffee shop, "was dazzled by the speed of his mind, although at times
I felt he sounded like a man on a public platform, and that much
of what he said had been said before" [Songlines, 11].) Utz, for example, ironizes one familiar quest narrative. It's "about the curse
of possessing the grail," writes Meanor, "because in this work the
problem is that Utz possesses his treasure" (129, emphasis original).
In Patagonia ironizes another: from Jason and the Golden Fleece
to Chatwin and the Reddish Sloth. No treasure. No Argo.[42]

Chatwin was equally obsessive about those notebooks. (Hemingway used carnets moleskines too, a connection Chatwin must have
recognized.) "Each time I went to Paris," he writes, "I would buy a
fresh supply from a papeterie in the Rue de l'Ancienne Comédie."

> The pages were squared and the end-papers held in place with
> an elastic band. I had numbered them in series. I wrote my
> name and address on the front page, offering a reward to the
> finder. To lose a passport was the least of one's worries: to lose a
> notebook was a catastrophe. (Songlines, 160)[43]

---

42. The Songlines contains an exception: a self-referential section about the generation of narrative form where Chatwin "becomes so profoundly engaged in his subject matter—which is nothing less than the dynamics of how words and music become a world—that he can no longer remain an objective collector of data or maintain a scholarly distance; he must enter the process" (Meanor, 109). The section—called "In the Beginning . . ."—represents the author's worst, least Flaubertian work. Then again, the narrator was drunk when he wrote it in some hotel room, presumably in bed.
43. This may be an allusion to Wilde. "To lose one parent, Mr. Worthing, may be regarded as a misfortune," says Lady Bracknell; "to lose both seems like carelessness" (Importance of Being Earnest, act 1, 500).

In fact, not all the pages are squared, by which Chatwin meant lined like graph paper. Some are lined in the usual way. Oddly enough, the lined notebooks have neatly written entries, the squared ones messy—or so it seems from two photographs in *Far Journeys* (King and Wyndham, 14–15). (When doesn't neatness count? As Chatwin remarked, on African graffiti: "Happily they are all in neat copybook handwriting and in French" ["Gone to Timbuctoo," in *Anatomy*, 31].) But whether or not this is true throughout, the entries themselves—as signifieds—are in fact messy, chaotic. Chatwin himself said the notebooks contain "a mishmash of nearly indecipherable jottings, 'thoughts,' quotations, brief encounters, travel notes, notes for stories" (*Songlines*, 75). Susannah Clapp, who edited *In Patagonia*, concurs: "The notebooks are an unstructured accumulation: records of conversations, reading-lists, descriptions of landscapes and people, quotations from books, chronicles of colors, line-drawings of doorways and arches, huge speculative statements, tiny anecdotes."

> They indicate how Chatwin trimmed and tucked and compressed his sentences before they got into print: they also show how little attention was sometimes necessary. They contain paragraphs with more flab than he would have allowed in a finished piece of work. But they also contain paragraphs which gain in verve because they have not been tooled over. They are lively fragments, musings, beginnings of ideas.

In sum, she says, there's "always a thin line between Bruce being brilliant and Bruce being batty" (Clapp, 204–5). (*The Songlines'* "From the Notebooks" section, claims Clapp, represents revision, not transcription; nor would Chatwin have included it had he been well enough to do the book properly. "Bruce" claims the section was written in that trailer.) Here, then, are the disarranged, disassembled pieces of those jigsaw puzzles—multiple games Chatwin played. Here then, his archive-like memory bank, unindexed. Here, true storytelling.

Neatness Counts, I've come to realize, has been the elegy for Steve I mentioned earlier. It reconfigures my own private derangement. It seeks to retrieve my irretrievable past. It retrieves our precomputer past as well. And so my brother, as represented, is the kind of solution for which Lydia Davis longs—one I've managed to discover not because I'm "clever" (her requirement), but because, like Barthes, I've read myself symptomatically. With that in mind, please permit—in closing—three quotations from the few texts I have in his hand (neatly written), or in his typewriting. (My own *Will to Power*.) They're not letters to me. I never got letters. Nor did he leave a note. They're from a file marked "David" and seem to reflect his truest self. A familiar self, though not disturbingly so. ("It is not in how one soul approaches another but in how it distances itself from it that I recognize their affinity and relatedness" [Nietzsche, 275].) A David of his own. Admire the writing if you like—I do—and try to remember how young he was at the time.

The first is a paper written for a class on androgyny. Titled "Two Expositions and Four Extenuations from 1975," it begins with an epigraph: "Whenever one loves another, which of the two becomes the friend of which, the lover of the loved one or the beloved of the loving one? Or does it not even make a difference? (Plato, *Lysis*)." Here's the first exposition:

> When I first saw David it was in September of 1974 and he was sitting on top of the multi-leveled sitting area in the lobby of Building Seven, on the highest level. There was some sort of noontime entertainment going on, although I don't remember what it was. I was hurrying out toward the Student Center for a quick lunch before going back to classes, and I probably never would have noticed him had he not been seated so prominently. His hair was longer then than it is today, and he seemed to be looking through his wire-rimmed glasses at nothing in particular, but in the general direction of the entertainers and the audience. I can remember stopping before I got to the doors, stepping aside out of the traffic, and staring at him (I think without him noticing me) for about forty-five seconds.
>
> Actually, I spend quite a bit of time just staring at all the beautiful faces at M.I.T. and lamenting the fact that because most of them belonged to other males, I would probably not be able to learn more about them than what one can learn from a distance of thirty feet and in only a few seconds. David's, however, seemed more important to me than the other faces, and not

just for the reason that his was the only one I was studying at the time. He has a way of looking at you that makes you feel as though he is in some mode of communication with you higher and more piercing than the verbal-intellectual one. When other people try to affect this they give you only vacant stares. His hair was smooth, but not shapelessly straight, and it was dark and unselfconsciously parted in the center; kempt enough to be attractive, but with a few wisps floating in the breeze to indicate casualness. His look was lean, but not hungry. His posture was unguarded and open, enough so that I didn't feel so lonely in staring at him. In physique he was and remains slim, not to the point of frailty, but in such a proportion to his body and stance as to make him as supple and yearning in appearance as Michelangelo's Adam.

An awful lot of thoughts went through my mind in those forty-five seconds. Everything about him suggested that he was my "type" but by this time I had pretty well become convinced that anyone I ever found appealing would be straight. Even though the statistics are more in my favor (about ten percent of the American white male population between the age of sixteen and death spend at least five years of their lives in a predominantly homosexual mode, and this is even higher for urban college youth in an experimental phase of life), I found that I was batting zero for finding anyone I really liked within that ten percent. Friends who noticed this attributed it to a fear of success, and I seriously wondered if they weren't right. The prospect of my never getting past this psychological barrier frustrated me, and I felt particularly bad about this while I was gazing at David. I also knew that I would never be able to forget him.

My brother Steve: a Barthesian cruiser, or flaneur, with a public posture of his own.

The second is a letter I assume he never sent.

I won't wax romantic about you as the only one I could ever love because it simply isn't true, I hope. Conversely, I wish you the very best of happiness with whomever you choose to wake up beside for the rest of your life. In other words, although I could seriously imagine spending the rest of my life with you (yes,

there is artificial intelligence in Israel), I know that such ideas
are merely dreams.

My brother Steve: a Flying Dutchman with his own semipublic
posture.

The third—more soliloquy than monologue—is from some
notebook. Stream-of-consciousness, rather.

> yes—because he touched me first—likes my writing—has the
> patience to sort through my pedantry—eyes that seem to say
> yes, but later—I have waited longer than I care to recall—we
> always get onto talking about my politics or his younger sister's
> rape or what a great place the Village is or his Fillmore West
> shirt—makes me think of all the places I'd like to visit with
> him—San Francisco is a great place to be alone with a friend
> or a lover—or just alone

Steve, in his own private derangement. A haunting presence.
Solitary.

FROM THE NOTEBOOKS

All the Little Flowers. The pronouncement, probably by Jean Paul, that memories are the only possessions which no one can take from us, belongs in the storehouse of impotently sentimental consolations that the subject, resignedly withdrawing into inwardness, would like to believe the very fulfillment that he has given up. In setting up his own archives, the subject seizes his own stock of experience as property, so making it something wholly external to himself. Past inner life is turned into furniture just as, conversely, every Biedermeier piece was memory made wood. The interior where the soul accommodates its collection of memoirs and curios is derelict. Memories cannot be conserved in drawers and pigeon-holes; in them the past is indissolubly woven into the present. No one has them at his disposal in the free and voluntary way that is praised in Jean Paul's fulsome sentences. Precisely where they become controllable and objectified, where the subject believes himself entirely sure of them, memories fade like delicate wallpapers in bright sunlight. But where, protected by oblivion, they keep their strength, they are endangered like all that is alive. This is why Bergson's and Proust's conception, intended to combat reification, that the present, immediacy, is constituted only through the mediation of memory, has not only a redeeming but an infernal aspect. Just as no earlier experience is real that has not been loosed by involuntary remembrance from the deathly fixity of its isolated existence, so conversely, no memory is guaranteed, existent in itself, indifferent to the future of him who harbors it; nothing past is proof, through its translation into mere imagination, against the curse of the empirical present. The most blissful memory of a person can be revoked in its very substance by later experience. He who has loved and who betrays love does harm not only to the image of the past, but to the past itself. Irresistibly evident, an impatient movement while waking up, a distraught tone of voice, a faint hypocrisy in pleasure, obtrudes itself in the memory and turns the earlier closeness even then into the distance that it has since become. Despair has the accent of irrevocability not because things cannot improve, but because it draws the past too into its vortex. Therefore it is foolish and sentimental to try to keep the past untainted by the present's turbid flood. No other hope is left to the past than that, exposed defenselessly to disaster, it shall emerge from it as something different. But he who dies in despair has lived his whole life in vain. (Adorno, *Minima Moralia*)

Jean Paul. Jean Paul knew a great deal but had no science, was skilled in all kinds of artistic artifices but had no art, found almost nothing unenjoyable but had no taste, possessed feeling and seriousness but when he offered a taste of them poured over them a repulsive broth of tears, he had indeed wit—but unhappily far too little to satisfy his ravenous hunger for it: which is why it is precisely through his lack of wit that he drives the reader to despair. On the whole he was a motley, strong-smelling weed that shot up overnight in the delicate fruitfields of Schiller and Goethe;

he was a complacent, good man, and yet a fatality—a fatality in a dressing-gown. (Nietzsche, *Human, All Too Human*)

Bad Books. A book ought to long for pen, ink, and writing-desk: but as a rule pen, ink, and writing-desk long for a book. That is why books are nowadays of so little account. (Nietzsche, *Human, All Too Human*)

Works Cited

Adorno, Theodor. *Minima Moralia: Reflections from Damaged Life.* Trans. E. F. N. Jephcott. London: Verso, 1978.

Albaret, Céleste. *Monsieur Proust.* Ed. Georges Belmont, trans. Barbara Bray. New York: McGraw-Hill, 1976.

Althusser, Louis. "Ideology and Ideological State Apparatuses (Notes towards an Investigation)." In *Lenin and Philosophy and Other Essays,* trans. Ben Brewster, 127–86. New York: Monthly Review Press, 1971.

Auster, Paul, and Sam Messer. *The Story of My Typewriter.* New York: D.A.P., 2002.

Bachelard, Gaston. *The Poetics of Space.* Trans. Maria Jolas. Boston: Beacon, 1994.

Barthes, Roland. "An Almost Obsessive Relation to Writing Instruments." In *The Grain of the Voice: Interviews, 1962–1980,* trans. Linda Coverdale, 177–82. New York: Hill and Wang, 1985.

———. "At Le Palace Tonight . . ." In *Incidents,* trans. Richard Howard, 43–48. Berkeley and Los Angeles: University of California Press, 1992.

———. *Camera Lucida.* Trans. Richard Howard. New York: Hill and Wang, 1981.

———. "Cy Twombly: Works on Paper." In *The Responsibility of Forms,* trans. Richard Howard, 157–76. New York: Hill and Wang, 1985.

———. "The Death of the Author." In *Image Music Text,* trans. Stephen Heath, 142–48. New York: Noonday, 1988.

———. "Deliberation." In *The Rustle of Language,* trans. Richard Howard, 359–73. New York: Hill and Wang, 1986.

———. *Empire of Signs.* Trans. Richard Howard. New York: Hill and Wang, 1982.

———. "From Work to Text." In *Image Music Text,* trans. Stephen Heath, 155–64. New York: Noonday, 1988.

———. "I Don't Believe in Influences." In *The Grain of the Voice: Interviews, 1962–1980,* trans. Linda Coverdale, 25–29. New York: Hill and Wang, 1985.

———. "Incidents." In *Incidents,* trans. Richard Howard, 11–41. Berkeley and Los Angeles: University of California Press, 1992.

———. *"Longtemps, je me suis couché de bonne heure . . . "* In *The Rustle of Language,* trans. Richard Howard, 277–90. New York: Hill and Wang, 1986.

———. *A Lover's Discourse: Fragments.* Trans. Richard Howard. New York: Hill and Wang, 1978.

———. "Masson's Semiography." In *The Responsibility of Forms,* trans. Richard Howard, 153–56. New York: Hill and Wang, 1985.

———. *Michelet.* Trans. Richard Howard. New York: Hill and Wang, 1987.

———. "Michelet's Modernity." In *The Rustle of Language,* trans. Richard Howard, 208–11. New York: Hill and Wang, 1986.

———. *Mythologies.* Trans. Annette Lavers. New York: Noonday, 1992.

———. "One Always Fails in Speaking of What One Loves." In *The Rustle of Language,* trans. Richard Howard, 296–305. New York: Hill and Wang, 1986.

———. *The Pleasure of the Text.* Trans. Richard Miller. New York: Hill and Wang, 1975.

———. "Pleasure/Writing/Reading." In *The Grain of the Voice: Interviews, 1962–1980,* trans. Linda Coverdale, 157–71. New York: Hill and Wang, 1985.

———. "Rasch." In *The Responsibility of Forms,* trans. Richard Howard, 299–312. New York: Hill and Wang, 1985.

———. *Roland Barthes by Roland Barthes.* Trans. Richard Howard. New York: Hill and Wang, 1977.

———. "Soirées de Paris." In *Incidents,* trans. Richard Howard, 49–73. Berkeley and Los Angeles: University of California Press, 1992.

———. "Style and Its Image." In *The Rustle of Language,* trans. Richard Howard, 90–99. New York: Hill and Wang, 1986.

———. "Twenty Key Words for Roland Barthes." In *The Grain of the Voice: Interviews, 1962–1980,* trans. Linda Coverdale, 205–32. New York: Hill and Wang, 1985.

———. *Writing Degree Zero.* Trans. Annette Lavers and Colin Smith. New York: Noonday, 1968.

Baudelaire, Charles. "Invitation au voyage." In *Les Fleurs du mal,* ed. Antoine Adam, 58–59. Paris: Garnier Frères, 1961. (Orig. pub. 1857.)

Benjamin, Walter. "A Berlin Chronicle." In *Reflections: Essays, Aphorisms, Autobiographical Writing,* ed. Peter Demetz, trans. Edmund Jephcott, 3–60. New York: Schocken, 1978.

———. *The Correspondence of Walter Benjamin, 1910–1940.* Ed. Gershom Scholem and Theodor W. Adorno, trans. Manfred R. Jacobson and Evelyn M. Jacobson. Chicago: University of Chicago Press, 1994.

———. "The Image of Proust." In *Illuminations: Essays and Reflections,* ed.

Hannah Arendt, trans. Harry Zohn, 201–15. New York: Schocken, 1985.

———. *Moscow Diary.* Ed. Gary Smith, trans. Richard Sieburth. Cambridge, Mass.: Harvard University Press, 1986.

———. "One-Way Street." In *Selected Writings,* vol. 1, *1913–1926,* ed. Marcus Bullock and Michael W. Jennings, trans. Edmund Jephcott, 444–88. Cambridge, Mass.: Harvard University Press, 1996.

———. "The Storyteller: Reflections on the Works of Nikolai Leskov." In *Illuminations: Essays and Reflections,* ed. Hannah Arendt, trans. Harry Zohn, 83–109. New York: Schocken, 1985.

———. "The Task of the Translator." In *Illuminations: Essays and Reflections,* ed. Hannah Arendt, trans. Harry Zohn, 69–82. New York: Schocken, 1985.

Bernstein, Richard. "Howard's Way." *New York Times Magazine,* September 25, 1988, 41–92.

Bishop, Elizabeth. *The Collected Prose.* Ed. Robert Giroux. New York: Farrar, Straus and Giroux, 1984.

———. *The Complete Poems, 1927–1979.* New York: Farrar, Straus and Giroux, 1983.

———. *One Art: Letters.* Ed. Robert Giroux. New York: Farrar, Straus and Giroux, 1994.

Blanchot, Maurice. *The Space of Literature.* Trans. Ann Smock. Lincoln: University of Nebraska Press, 1982.

Bolz, Norbert, and Willem van Reijen. *Walter Benjamin.* Trans. Laimdota Mazzarins. Atlantic Highlands, N.J.: Humanities Press, 1996.

Bonaparte, Marie. *The Life and Works of Edgar Allan Poe.* London: Imago, 1949.

Brater, Enoch. "Tom Stoppard's Brit/Lit/Crit." In *The Cambridge Companion to Tom Stoppard,* ed. Katherine E. Kelly, 203–12. Cambridge: Cambridge University Press, 2001.

Brodersen, Momme. *Walter Benjamin: A Biography.* Ed. Martina Dervis, trans. Malcolm R. Green and Ingrida Ligers. London: Verso, 1996.

Bull, John. "Tom Stoppard and Politics." In *The Cambridge Companion to Tom Stoppard,* ed. Katherine E. Kelly, 136–53. Cambridge: Cambridge University Press, 2001.

Burke, Séan. *The Death and Return of the Author: Criticism and Subjectivity in Barthes, Foucault, and Derrida.* Edinburgh: Edinburgh University Press, 1998.

Calasso, Roberto. "Chette-Wynde." Trans. Avril Bardoni. In *Winding Paths: Photographs by Bruce Chatwin,* 9–15. London: Jonathan Cape, 1999.

Callen, Anthea. *The Spectacular Body: Science, Method, and Meaning in the Work of Degas*. New Haven, Conn.: Yale University Press, 1995.

Chartier, Roger, ed. *A History of Private Life,* vol. 3, *Passions of the Renaissance*. Cambridge, Mass.: Harvard University Press, 1989.

Chatwin, Bruce. *Anatomy of Restlessness: Selected Writings, 1969–1989*. New York: Penguin, 1996.

———. *Far Journeys: Photographs and Notebooks*. Ed. David King and Francis Wyndham. New York: Viking, 1993.

———. *In Patagonia*. New York: Penguin, 1988.

———. *On the Black Hill*. New York: Penguin, 1984.

———. *The Songlines*. New York: Penguin, 1988.

———. *Utz*. New York: Penguin, 1989.

———. *What Am I Doing Here*. New York: Penguin, 1990.

Clapp, Susannah. *With Chatwin: Portrait of a Writer*. New York: Knopf, 1997.

Cocteau, Jean. *Past Tense,* vol. 1, *Diaries*. Trans. Richard Howard. New York: Harcourt Brace Jovanovich, 1987.

Collins, Billy. *The Apple That Astonished Paris*. Fayetteville: University of Arkansas Press, 1988.

———. *The Art of Drowning*. Pittsburgh, Pa.: University of Pittsburgh Press, 1995.

Cramer, Steven. "Freud's Desk, Vienna, 1938." *Ploughshares* 9.1 (Spring 1983): 125–26.

Davis, Lydia. *The End of the Story*. New York: High Risk, 1995.

Delaney, Paul. "Exit Tomás Sträussler, Enter Sir Tom Stoppard." In *The Cambridge Companion to Tom Stoppard,* ed. Katherine E. Kelly, 25–37. Cambridge: Cambridge University Press, 2001.

Delany, Samuel R. *The Motion of Light in Water: Sex and Science Fiction Writing in the East Village: 1960–1965*. New York: Richard Kasak, 1993. Reprint, Minneapolis: University of Minnesota Press, 2004. Page references are to the 1993 edition.

Derrida, Jacques. *The Work of Mourning*. Ed. Pascale-Anne Brault and Michael Naas. Chicago: University of Chicago Press, 2001.

Dillard, Annie. *The Writing Life*. New York: HarperPerennial, 1990.

Disch, Thomas M. "Getting into Death." In *Getting into Death: The Best Short Stories of Thomas M. Disch,* 177–206. London: Hart-Davis, MacGibbon, 1973.

Doreski, C. K. "Proustian Closure in Wallace Steven's 'The Rock' and Elizabeth Bishop's *Geography III*." *Twentieth-Century Literature* 44.1 (Spring 1998): 34–52.

Doty, Mark, ed. *Open House: Writers Redefine Home.* Saint Paul, Minn.: Graywolf Press, 2003.

Drucker, Hal, and Sid Lerner. *From the Desk Of.* New York: Harcourt Brace Jovanovich, 1989.

Eliot, George. *Middlemarch.* London: Zodiac, 1978: (Orig. pub. 1871–72.)

Enzensberger, Hans Magnus. "Much Left Unsaid." *Times Literary Supplement,* June 16, 1989, 657.

Fiffer, Sharon Sloan, and Steve Fiffer. *Home: American Writers Remember Rooms of Their Own.* New York: Vintage, 1995.

Fleming, John. *Stoppard's Theater: Finding Order amid Chaos.* Austin: University of Texas Press, 2001.

Foucault, Michel. *The Order of Things.* New York: Vintage, 1973.

———. *This Is Not a Pipe.* Trans. James Harkness. Berkeley and Los Angeles: University of California Press, 1983.

Freud, Sigmund. "Character and Anal Erotism." In *Character and Culture,* ed. Phillip Rieff, trans. R. C. McWatters, 27–33. New York: Collier, 1963.

———. "The Uncanny." Trans. James Strachey. In *Literary Theory: An Anthology,* ed. Julie Rivkin and Michael Ryan, 154–67. Oxford: Blackwell, 1998.

Fuss, Diana. *The Sense of an Interior.* New York: Routledge, 2004.

Genette, Gérard. *Narrative Discourse: An Essay in Method.* Trans. Jane E. Lewin. Ithaca, N.Y.: Cornell University Press, 1980.

Gide, André. *Incidences.* Paris: Gallimard, 1924.

———. *The Journals of André Gide.* Trans. Justin O'Brien. 4 vols. New York: Knopf, 1947–51.

Gladwell, Malcolm. "The Social Life of Paper." Review of *The Myth of the Paperless Office,* by Abigail Sellen and Richard Harper. *New Yorker,* March 25, 2002, 92–96.

Goldberg, Jonathan. *Writing Matter: From the Hands of the English Renaissance.* Stanford, Calif.: Stanford University Press, 1990.

Goldensohn, Lorrie. *Elizabeth Bishop: The Biography of a Poetry.* New York: Columbia University Press, 1992.

Gritten, David. "Damned Allusive Pimpernel." *Evening Standard,* May 19, 1984, 29.

Guppy, Shusha. "Tom Stoppard: The Art of Theater VII." In *Tom Stoppard in Conversation,* ed. Paul Delaney, 177–92. Ann Arbor: University of Michigan Press, 1993.

Gussow, Mel. *Conversations with Stoppard.* New York: Grove, 1995.

Hammer, Langdon. "Useless Concentration: Life and Work in Elizabeth

Bishop's Letters and Poems." *American Literary History* 9.1 (Spring 1997): 162–80.

Harlow, Barbara J. *Marcel Proust: A Study in Translation.* Buffalo: State University of New York at Buffalo, 1977.

Hayles, N. Katherine. *Chaos Bound: Orderly Disorder in Contemporary Literature and Science.* Ithaca, N.Y.: Cornell University Press, 1990.

Howard, Richard. "From *In Search of Lost Time.*" *Paris Review* 111 (1989): 14–33.

———. *Like Most Revelations.* New York: Pantheon, 1994.

———. "Translator's Note." In *Critical Essays,* by Roland Barthes, trans. Richard Howard, ix–x. Evanston, Ill.: Northwestern University Press, 1972.

Hudson, Roger, Catherine Itzin, and Simon Trussler. "Ambushes for the Audience: Towards a High Comedy of Ideas." In *Tom Stoppard in Conversation,* ed. Paul Delaney, 51–72. Ann Arbor: University of Michigan Press, 1993.

Ignatieff, Michael. "An Interview with Bruce Chatwin." *Granta* 21 (Spring 1987): 22–37.

Kael, Pauline. *I Lost It at the Movies.* Boston: Little, Brown, 1965.

Kalstone, David. *Becoming a Poet: Elizabeth Bishop with Marianne Moore and Robert Lowell.* Ed. Robert Hemenway. Ann Arbor: University of Michigan Press, 2001.

Kelly, Katherine E. "Introduction: Tom Stoppard in Transformation." In *The Cambridge Companion to Tom Stoppard,* ed. Katherine E. Kelly, 10–22. Cambridge: Cambridge University Press, 2001.

King, David, and Francis Wyndham, eds. *Far Journeys: Photographs and Notebooks/Bruce Chatwin.* New York: Viking, 1993.

King, Stephen. *On Writing: A Memoir of the Craft.* New York: Pocket, 2000.

Koestenbaum, Wayne. "Logorrhea." *Southwest Review* 79.1 (Winter 1994): 102–6.

Kopelson, Kevin. *Beethoven's Kiss: Pianism, Perversion, and the Mastery of Desire.* Stanford, Calif.: Stanford University Press, 1996.

———. *Love's Litany: The Writing of Modern Homoerotics.* Stanford, Calif.: Stanford University Press, 1994.

———. *The Queer Afterlife of Vaslav Nijinsky.* Stanford, Calif.: Stanford University Press, 1997.

———. "Wilde, Barthes, and the Orgasmics of Truth." *Genders* 7 (March 1990): 22–31.

Krementz, Jill. *The Writer's Desk.* New York: Random House, 1996.

Kristeva, Julia. *Powers of Horror: An Essay on Abjection.* Trans. Leon Roudiez. New York: Columbia University Press, 1982.

———. *Revolution in Poetic Language.* Trans. Margaret Waller. New York: Columbia University Press, 1984.

———. *Time and Sense: Proust and the Experience of Literature.* Trans. Ross Guberman. New York: Columbia University Press, 1996.

———. "Word, Dialogue, and Novel." Trans. Alice Jardine, Thomas Gora, and Leon Roudiez. In *The Kristeva Reader,* ed. Toril Moi, 34–61. Oxford: Blackwell, 1986.

Lacan, Jacques. "The Seminar on 'The Purloined Letter.'" Trans. Jeffrey Mehlman. *Yale French Studies* 48 (1973): 39–72.

Ladenson, Elizabeth. *Proust's Lesbianism.* Ithaca, N.Y.: Cornell University Press, 1999.

Lanham, Fritz. "Poet Says Grant Won't Alter His Life." *Houston Chronicle,* June 20, 1996.

Laplanche, Jean, and Jean-Bertrand Pontalis. "Fantasy and the Origins of Sexuality." In *Formations of Fantasy,* ed. Victor Burgin, James Donald, and Cora Kaplan, 5–34. London: Methuen, 1986.

Lee, Josephine. "*In the Native State* and *Indian Ink.*" In *The Cambridge Companion to Tom Stoppard,* ed. Katherine E. Kelly, 38–52. Cambridge: Cambridge University Press, 2001.

Levenson, Jill L. "Stoppard's Shakespeare: Textual Revisions." In *The Cambridge Companion to Tom Stoppard,* ed. Katherine E. Kelly, 154–70. Cambridge: Cambridge University Press, 2001.

Levinson, Marjorie. "Picturing Pleasure: Some Poems by Elizabeth Bishop." In *What's Left of Theory? New Work on the Politics of Literary Theory,* ed. Judith Butler, John Guillory, and Kendall Thomas, 192–239. New York: Routledge, 2000.

Lipsky-Karasz, Elisa. "*Bazaar* Moments: Cloning Home." *Harper's Bazaar,* December 2001, 73.

Litvak, Joseph. *Strange Gourmets: Sophistication, Theory, and the Novel.* Durham, N.C.: Duke University Press, 1997.

Lombardi, Marilyn May. *The Body and the Song: Elizabeth Bishop's Poetics.* Carbondale: Southern Illinois University Press, 1995.

Mann, Thomas. *Death in Venice.* Trans. Stanley Appelbaum. New York: Dover, 1995. (Orig. pub. 1913.)

Mares, Cheryl. "Woolf's Reading of Proust." In *Reading Proust Now,* ed. Mary Ann Caws and Eugène Nicole, 185–95. New York: Peter Lang, 1990.

Marowitz, Charles. "Tom Stoppard: The Theater's Intellectual P. T. Barnum." *New York Times,* October 19, 1975, sec. 2.

McCabe, Susan. *Elizabeth Bishop: Her Poetics of Loss.* University Park: Pennsylvania State University Press, 1994.

McEwen, John. *Shapes on the Horizon: Teddy Millington-Drake.* London: Hobhouse, 1996.

Mead, Rebecca. "A Home-Ec Bible and W. H. Auden." *New Yorker,* March 20, 2000, 46–48.

Meanor, Patrick. *Bruce Chatwin.* New York: Twayne, 1997.

Millier, Brett C. *Elizabeth Bishop: Life and the Memory of It.* Berkeley and Los Angeles: University of California Press, 1993.

Monteiro, George, ed. *Conversations with Elizabeth Bishop.* Jackson: University Press of Mississippi, 1996.

Murdoch, Iris. "The Sublime and the Beautiful Revisited." *Yale Review* 49 (1959): 247–71.

Nadel, Ira. *Tom Stoppard: A Life.* New York: Palgrave, 2002.

Nancy, Jean-Luc. "Dum Scribo." *Oxford Literary Review* 3.2 (1978): 6–21.

Nietzsche, Friedrich. *Human, All Too Human.* Trans. R. J. Hollingdale. Cambridge: Cambridge University Press, 1996. (Orig. pub. 1878–86.)

Ockman, Carol. *Ingres's Eroticized Bodies: Retracing the Serpentine Line.* New Haven, Conn.: Yale University Press, 1995.

Ophir, Adi. "A Place of Knowledge Re-created: The Library of Michel de Montaigne." *Science in Context* 4.1 (1991): 163–89.

Orr, Mary. *Flaubert: Writing the Masculine.* Oxford: Oxford University Press, 2000.

Painter, George D. *Marcel Proust: A Biography.* 2 vols. New York: Vintage, 1978.

Pelz, Annegret. "The Desk: Excavation Site and Repository of Memories." Trans. and revised by Anne Puetz. In *Producing the Past: Aspects of Antiquarian Culture and Practice, 1700–1850,* ed. Martin Myrone and Lucy Pelz, 135–47. Brookfield, Vt.: Ashgate, 1999.

Poirier, Richard. "In Praise of Mess." Review of *With Walt Whitman in Camden,* vol. 7, *February 11, 1891–September 30, 1891*; vol. 9, *October 1, 1891–April 3, 1892,* by Horace Traubel, ed. Jeanne Chapman and Robert MacIsaac. *London Review of Books* 20.11 (June 4, 1998): 20–23.

Proust, Marcel. *In Search of Lost Time.* Trans. C. K. Scott Moncrieff and Terence Kilmartin. Revised by D. J. Enright. 6 vols. New York: Modern Library, 1992.

———. *On Reading.* Trans. and ed. Jean Autret and William Burford. New York: Macmillan, 1971.

Rabinowitz, Peter J. "Narrative Difficulties in *Lord Malquist and Mr.*

Moon." In *The Cambridge Companion to Tom Stoppard,* ed. Katherine E. Kelly, 55–67. Cambridge: Cambridge University Press, 2001.

Remnick, David. "Into the Clear." *New Yorker,* May 8, 2000, 76–89.

Ronell, Avital. *Stupidity.* Urbana and Chicago: University of Illinois Press, 2001.

Rose, Phyllis. *The Year of Reading Proust: A Memoir in Real Time.* New York: Scribner, 1997.

Rushdie, Salman. "Chatwin's Travels." In *Imaginary Homelands: Essays and Criticism, 1981–1991,* 237–40. London: Granta, 1991.

———. "Traveling with Chatwin." In *Imaginary Homelands: Essays and Criticism, 1981–1991,* 232–36. London: Granta, 1991.

Sammells, Neil. "The Early Stage Plays." In *The Cambridge Companion to Tom Stoppard,* ed. Katherine E. Kelly, 104–19. Cambridge: Cambridge University Press, 2001.

Sanders, Joel, and Diana Fuss. "Berggasse 19: Inside Freud's Office." In *Stud: Architectures of Masculinity,* ed. Joel Sanders, 112–39. New York: Princeton Architectural Press, 1996.

Schehr, Lawrence R. *"Les Offices de Flaubert: Étude bureaugraphie."* *Milieux* 32 (1988): 60–65.

Schiff, Stephen. "Full Stoppard." In *Stoppard in Conversation,* ed. Paul Delaney, 212–24. Ann Arbor: University of Michigan Press, 1994.

Sedgwick, Eve Kosofsky. *Epistemology of the Closet.* Berkeley and Los Angeles: University of California Press, 1990.

Shakespeare, Nicholas. *Bruce Chatwin.* New York: Anchor, 2001.

Smith, Paul. *Discerning the Subject.* Minneapolis: University of Minnesota Press, 1988.

Spacks, Patricia Meyer. *Boredom: The Literary History of a State of Mind.* Chicago: University of Chicago Press, 1995.

Spiegelman, Willard. "Landscape and Knowledge: The Poetry of Elizabeth Bishop." *Modern Poetry Studies* 6.3 (Winter 1975): 203–24.

Spires, Elizabeth. "The Art of Poetry XXVII." *Paris Review* 23 (Summer 1981): 57–83.

Steiner, George. *After Babel: Aspects of Language and Translation.* Oxford: Oxford University Press, 1992.

Stevenson, Anne. *Elizabeth Bishop.* New York: Twayne, 1966.

———. *Five Looks at Elizabeth Bishop.* London: Bellew, 1998.

Stoppard, Tom. *Arcadia.* London: Faber and Faber, 1993.

———. "But for the Middle Classes." Review of *Enemies of Society,* by Paul Johnson. *Times Literary Supplement,* June 3, 1977, 677.

———. *The Invention of Love.* New York: Grove, 1998.

———. *Jumpers.* New York: Grove, 1973.

———. *Plays.* 5 vols. London: Faber and Faber, 1996–99.

———. *Travesties.* New York: Grove, 1975.

Tadié, Jean–Yves. *Marcel Proust.* Trans. Euan Cameron. New York: Viking, 2000.

Thornton, Dora. *The Scholar in His Study: Ownership and Experience in Renaissance Italy.* New Haven, Conn.: Yale University Press, 1997.

Travisano, Thomas J. *Elizabeth Bishop: Her Artistic Development.* Charlottesville: University Press of Virginia, 1988.

Trotter, David. *Cooking with Mud: The Idea of Mess in Nineteenth-Century Art and Fiction.* Oxford: Oxford University Press, 2000.

Vendler, Helen. "Domestication, Domesticity, and the Otherworldly." In *Elizabeth Bishop and Her Art,* ed. Lloyd Schwartz and Sybil Estess, 32–48. Ann Arbor: University of Michigan Press, 1983.

Vigne, Georges. *Ingres.* Trans. John Goodman. New York: Abbeville, 1995.

Watson, Janell. *Literature and Material Culture from Balzac to Proust: The Collection and Consumption of Curiosities.* Cambridge: Cambridge University Press, 1999.

Whitaker, Thomas R. *Tom Stoppard.* New York: Grove, 1993.

Wilde, Oscar. "The Critic as Artist." In *The Artist as Critic: Critical Writings of Oscar Wilde,* ed. Richard Ellmann, 341–408. Chicago: University of Chicago Press, 1968.

———. *The Importance of Being Earnest.* In *The Complete Illustrated Stories, Plays, and Poems of Oscar Wilde,* 488–534. London: Chancellor, 1986. (Orig. pub. 1895.)

Woolf, Virginia. *The Diary of Virginia Woolf.* Ed. Anne Olivier Bell. 5 vols. New York: Harcourt Brace Jovanovich, 1977–84.

———. *The Letters of Virginia Woolf.* Ed. Nigel Nicolson. 6 vols. New York: Harcourt Brace Jovanovich, 1975–80.

———. Manuscript Notes and Drafts for "Phases of Fiction." B.6d. Monk's House Papers. University of Sussex Library.

———. "Phases of Fiction." In *Granite and Rainbow: Essays,* 93–145. New York: Hogarth, 1960.

Wyndham, Francis. "Introduction." In *Far Journeys: Photographs and Notebooks/Bruce Chatwin,* ed. David King and Francis Wyndham, 10–13. New York: Viking, 1993.

Yoshimoto, Banana. *N.P.* Trans. Ann Sherif. New York: Washington Square, 1994.

Yourcenar, Marguerite. *With Open Eyes: Conversations with Matthieu Galey.* Trans. Arthur Goldhammer. Boston: Beacon, 1984.

Zeifman, Hersh. "The Comedy of Eros: Stoppard in Love." In *The Cambridge Companion to Tom Stoppard,* ed. Katherine E. Kelly, 185–200. Cambridge: Cambridge University Press, 2001.

Zinman, Toby. *"Travesties, Night and Day, The Real Thing."* In *The Cambridge Companion to Tom Stoppard,* ed. Katherine E. Kelly, 120–35. Cambridge: Cambridge University Press, 2001.

INDEX

Kevin Kopelson is professor of English at the University of Iowa. He is author of *The Queer Afterlife of Vaslav Nijinsky, Beethoven's Kiss: Pianism, Perversion, and the Mastery of Desire,* and *Love's Litany: The Writing of Modern Homoerotics.*